"LOVE ME. LOVE MY TEDDY BEAR."

"LOVE ME. LOVE MY TEDDY BEAR."

S. GROSS

A Perigee Book

Perigee Books
are published by
The Putnam Publishing Group
200 Madison Avenue
New York, NY 10016

Published simultaneously in Canada by
General Publishing Co. Limited, Toronto

ISBN 0-399-51230-6

Printed in the United States of America

1 2 3 4 5 6 7 8 9 10

This book is dedicated to my nephew,
Andrew.
(*Now get off my back, Andy.*)

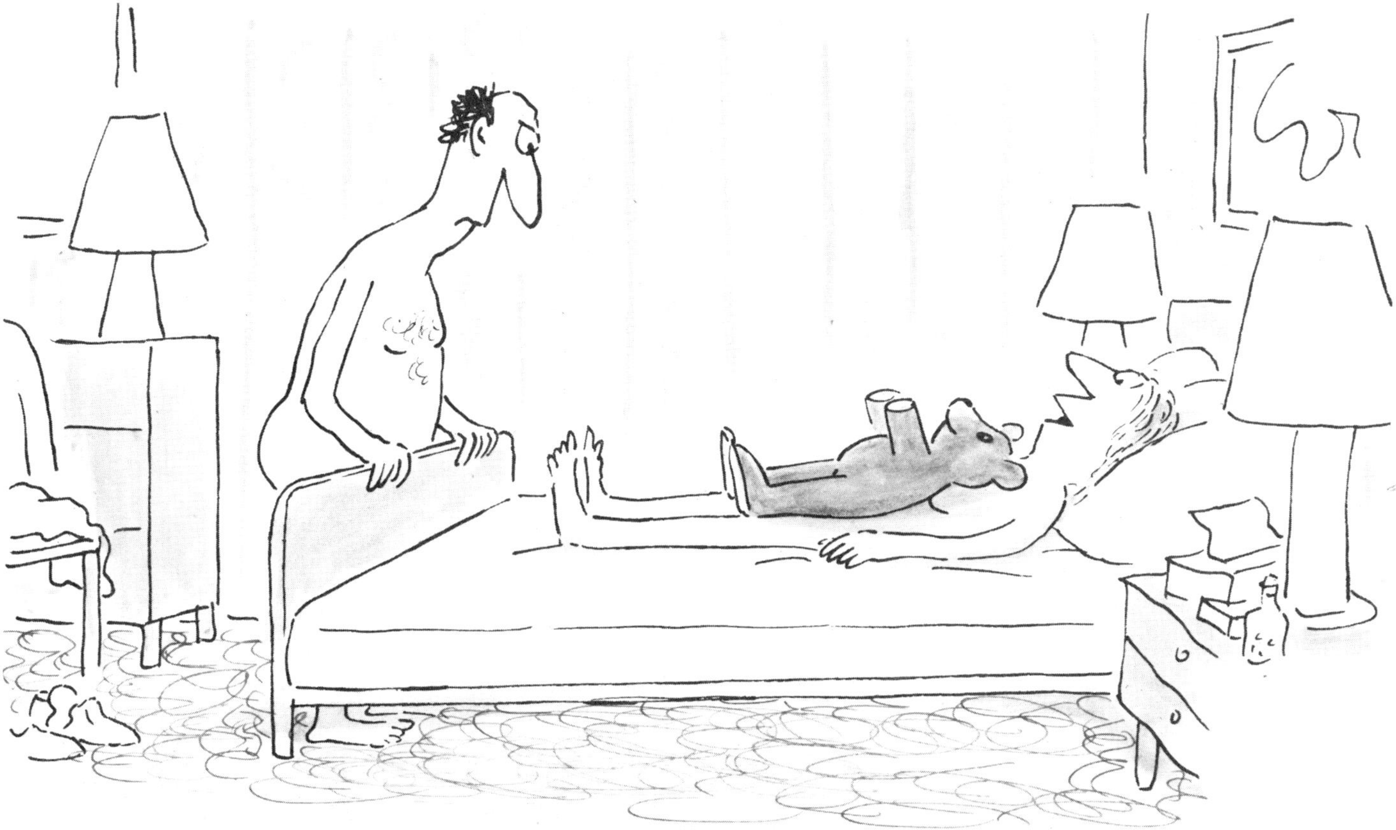

"Love me. Love my teddy bear."

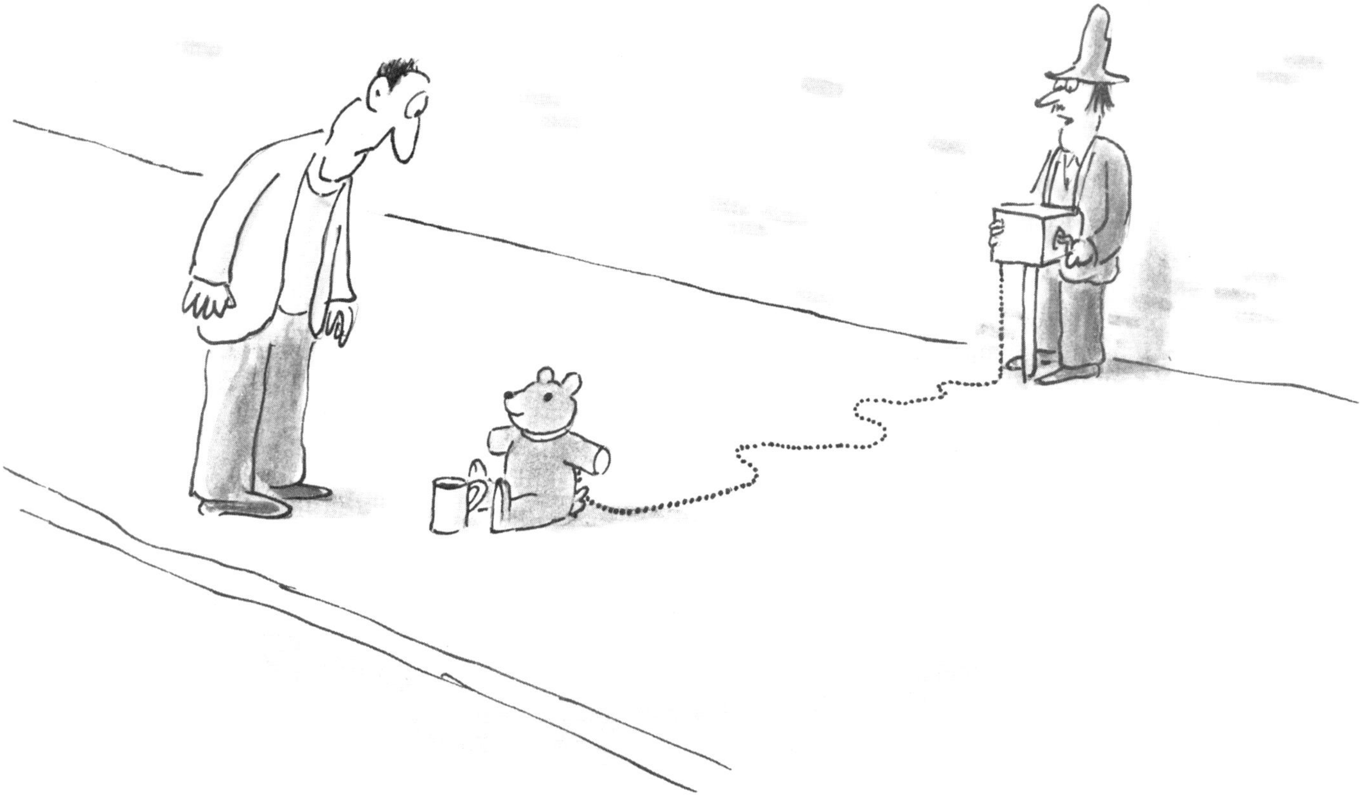

"My monkey died."

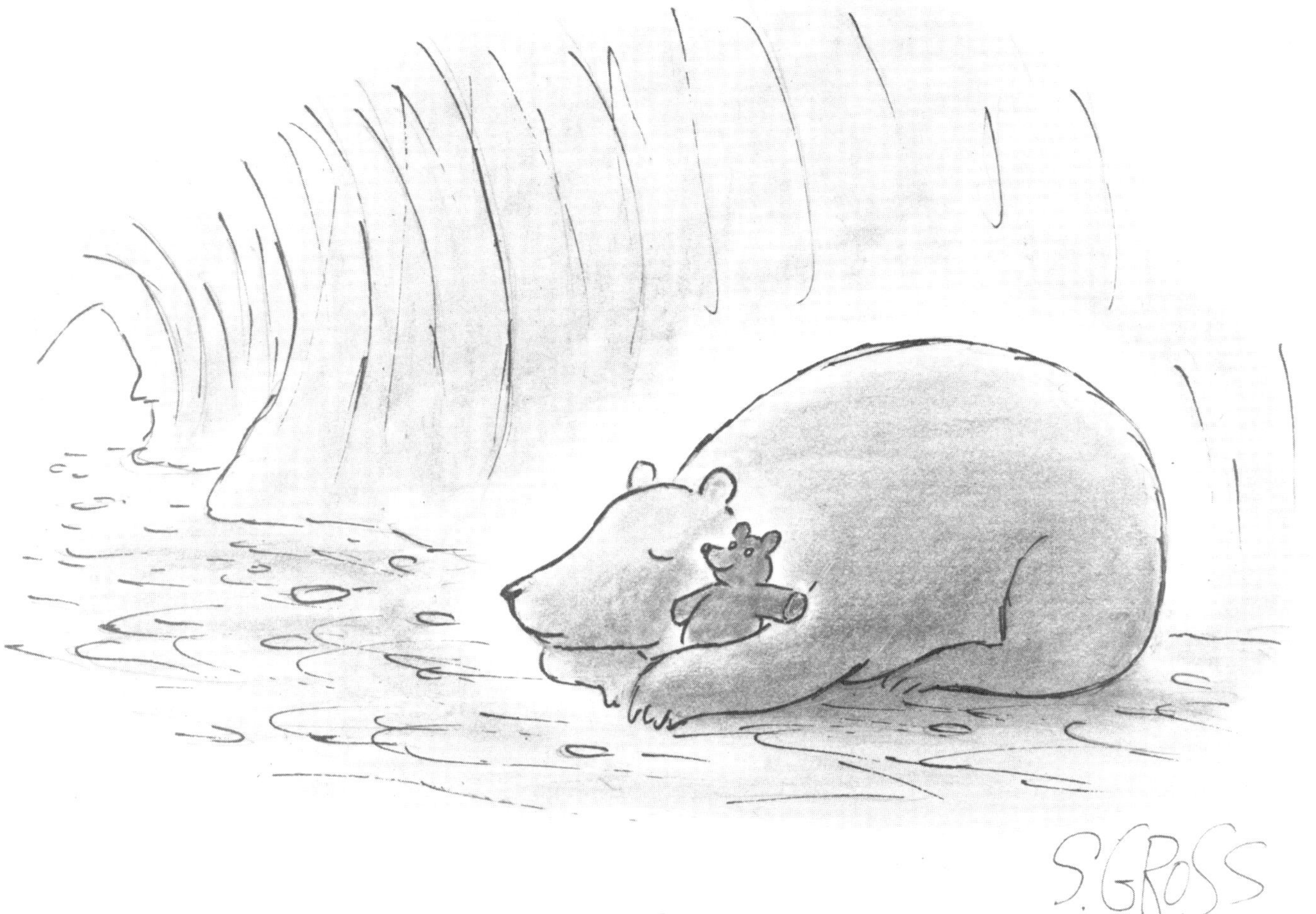
S.GROSS

"I thought it would taste like bear meat, but it doesn't."

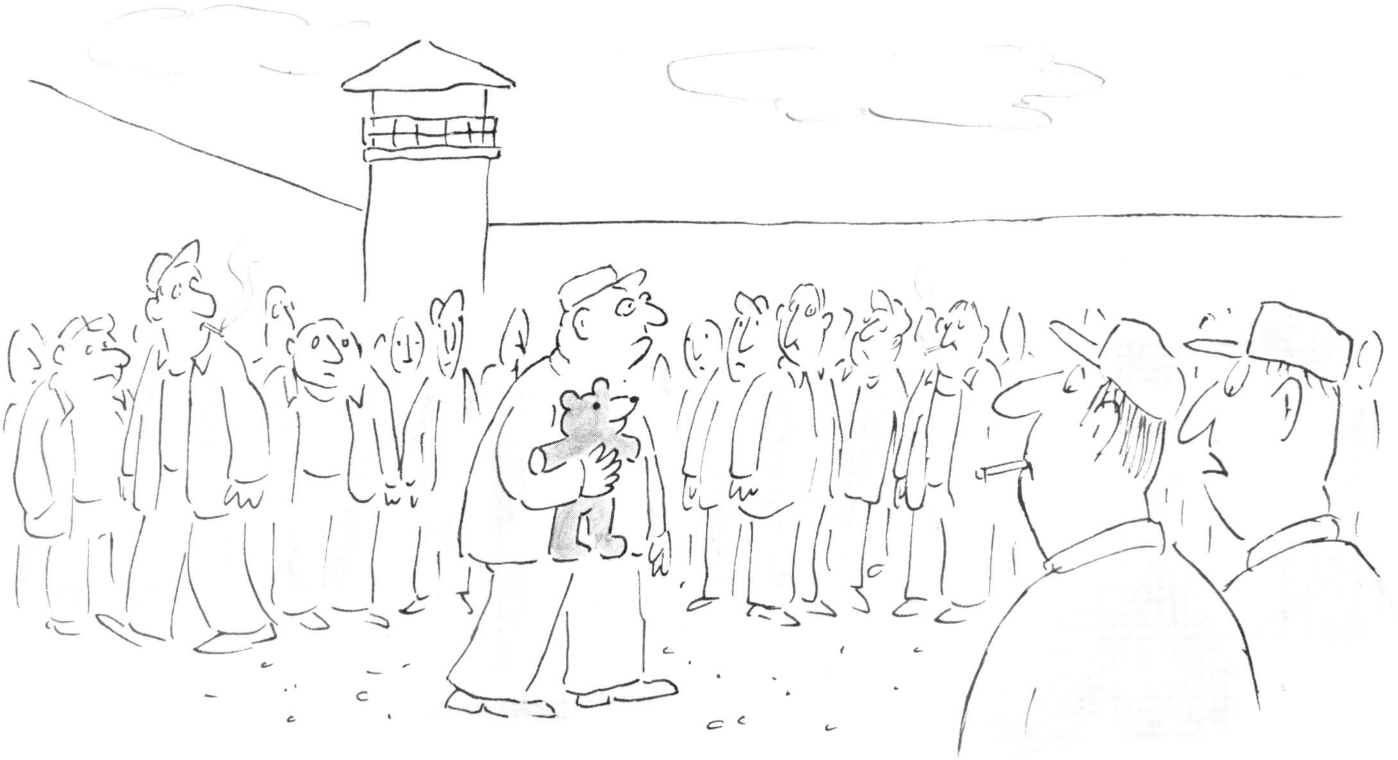

"He's either very, very tough or very, very crazy."

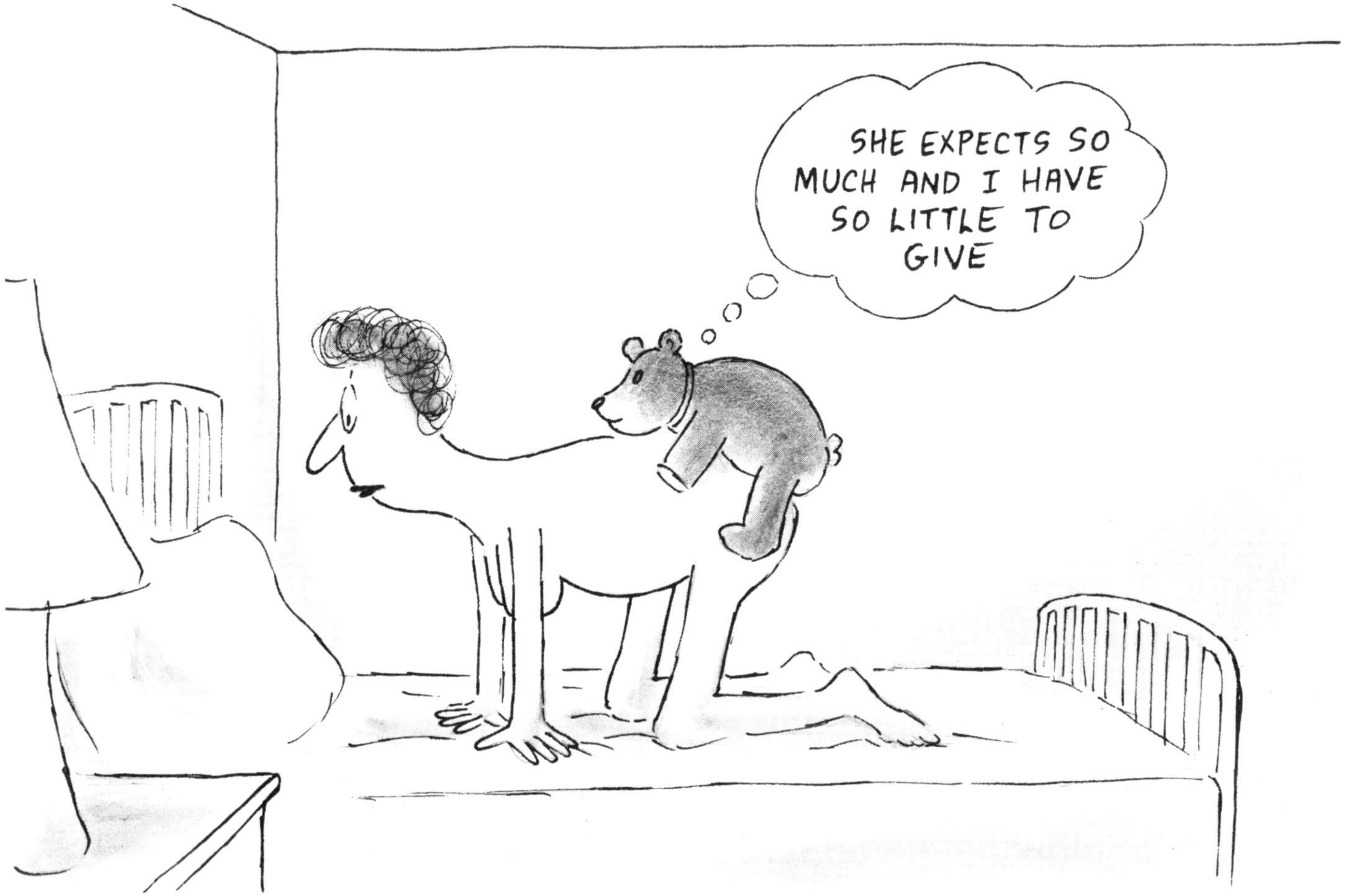
SHE EXPECTS SO MUCH AND I HAVE SO LITTLE TO GIVE

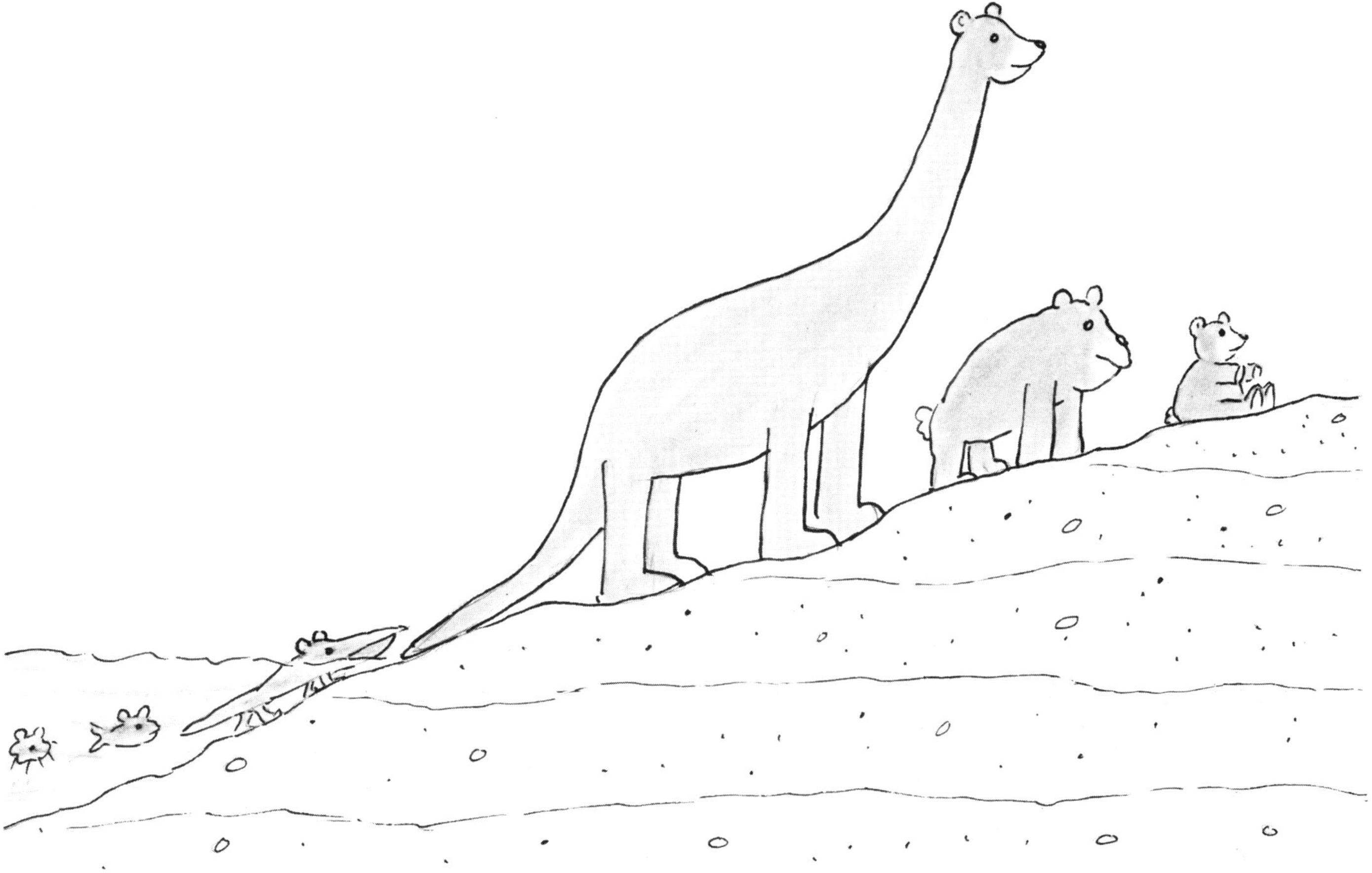

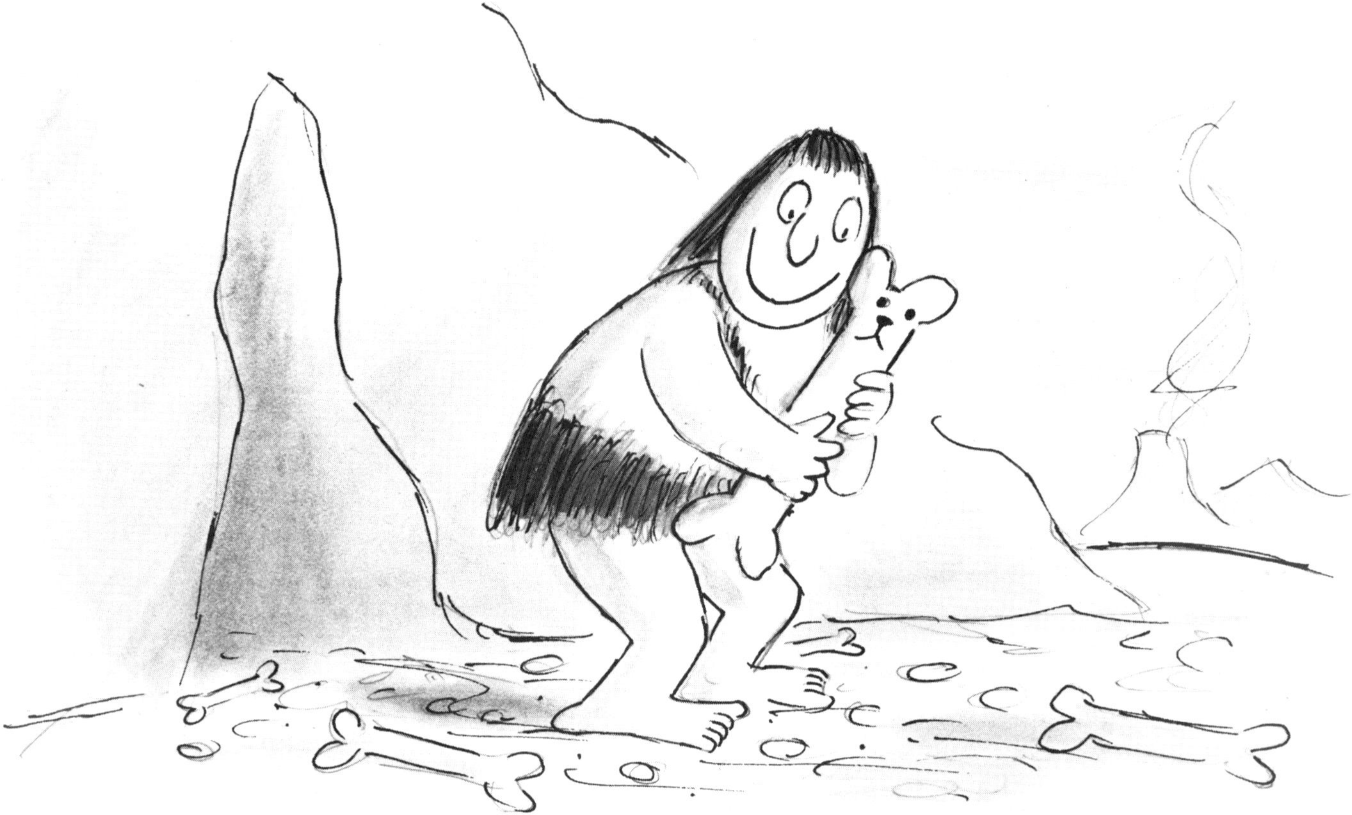

Prehistoric Teddy Bear

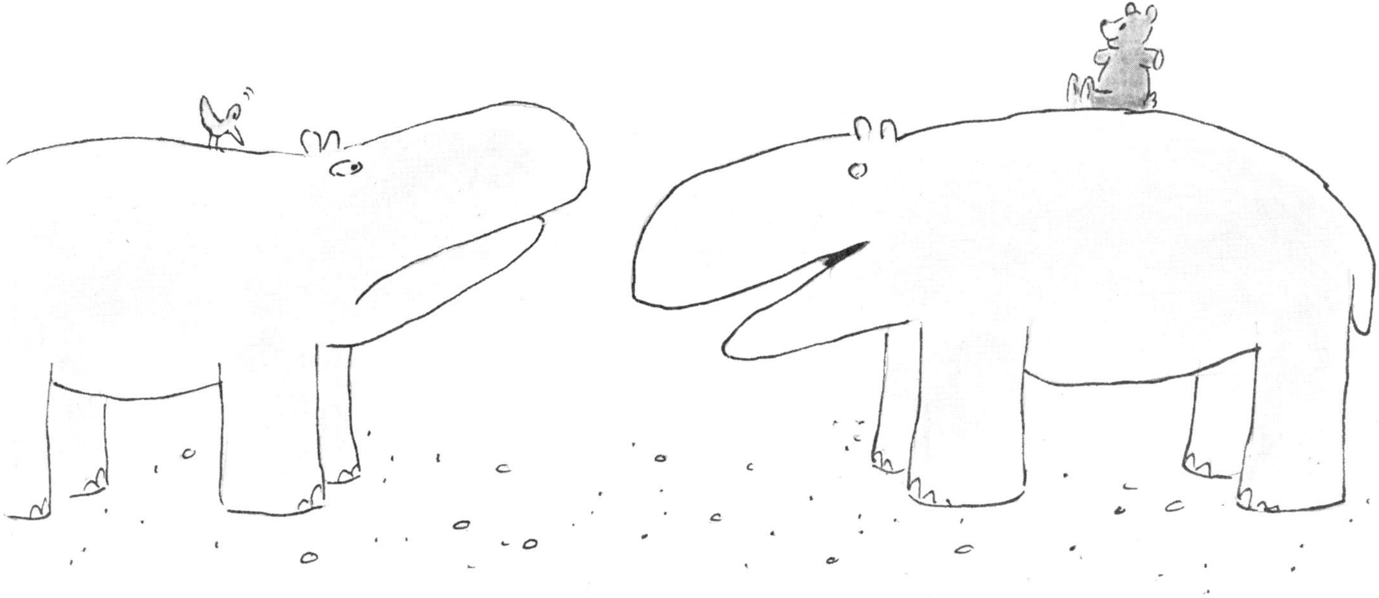

"I don't need a symbiotic relationship. I have Fred."

"It's the only way I can get him to drink milk."

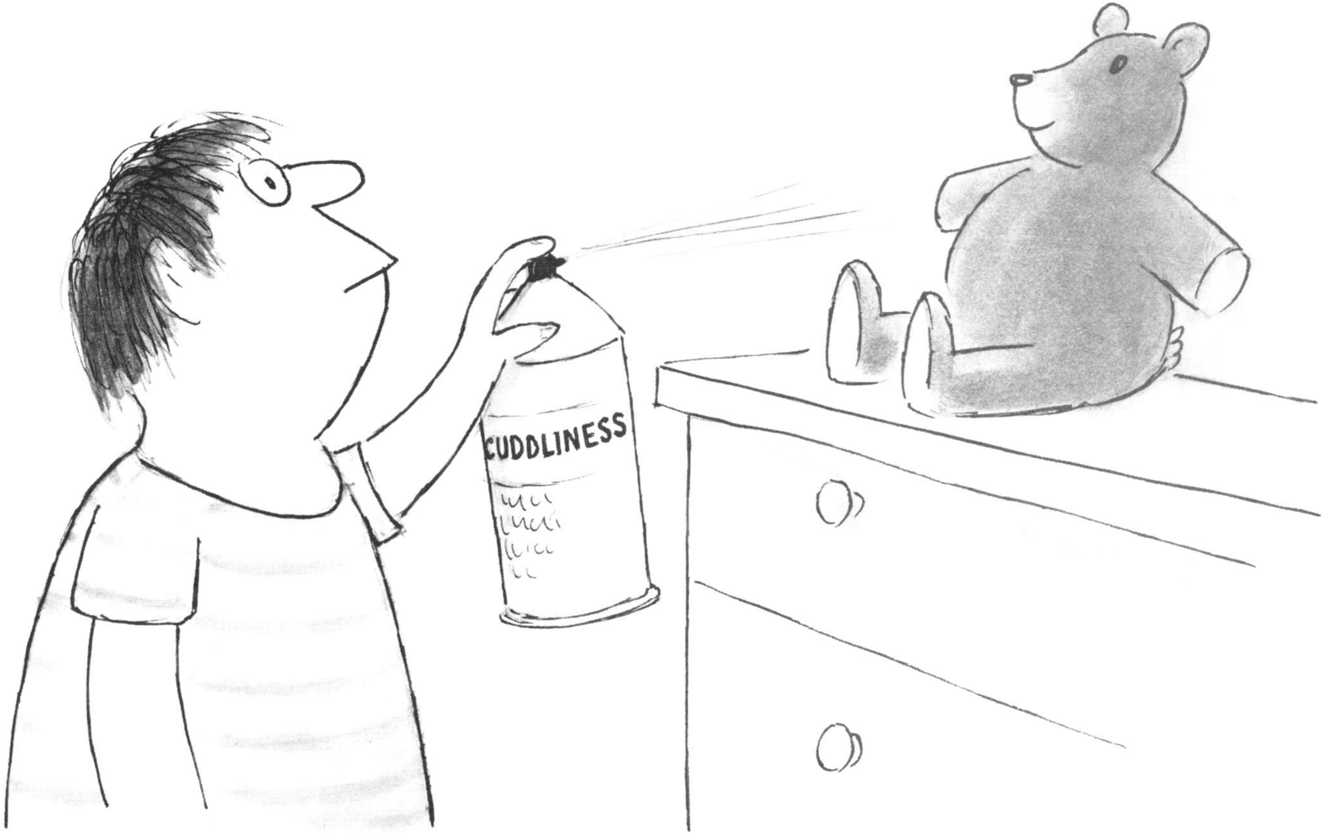
CUDDLINESS

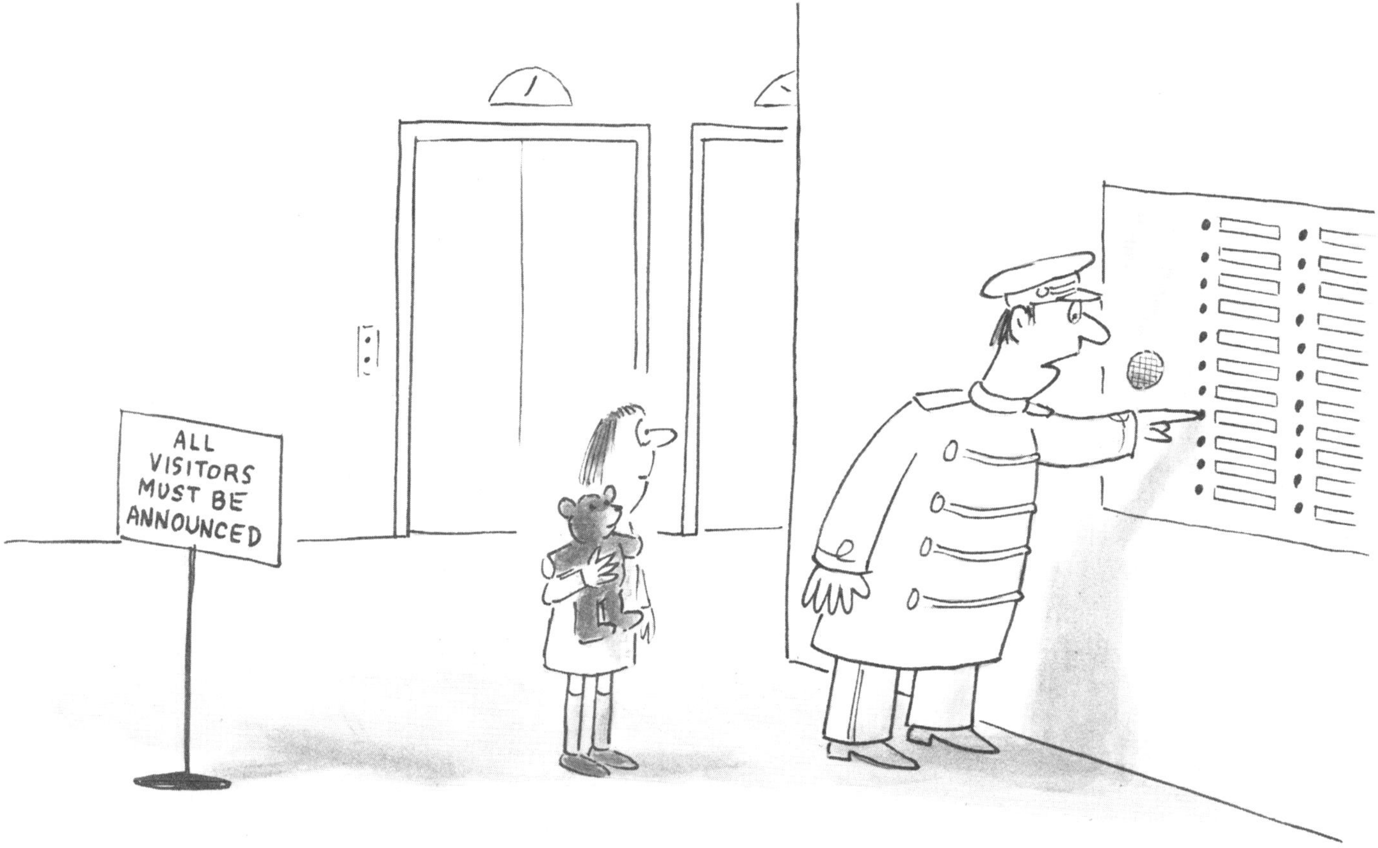
ALL VISITORS MUST BE ANNOUNCED

"Jennifer and 'Huggy Poo.'"

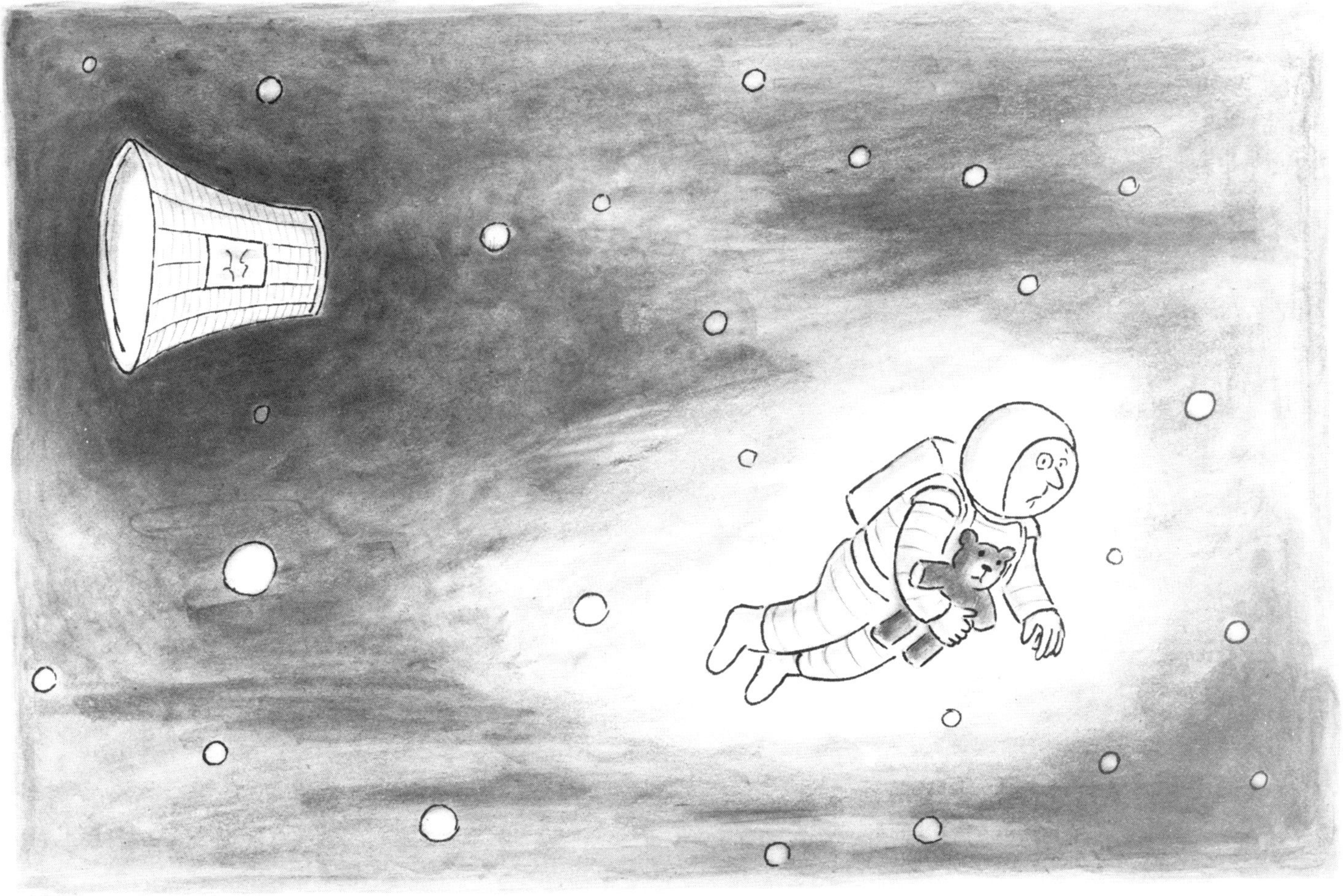

Helen Keller's Teddy Bear

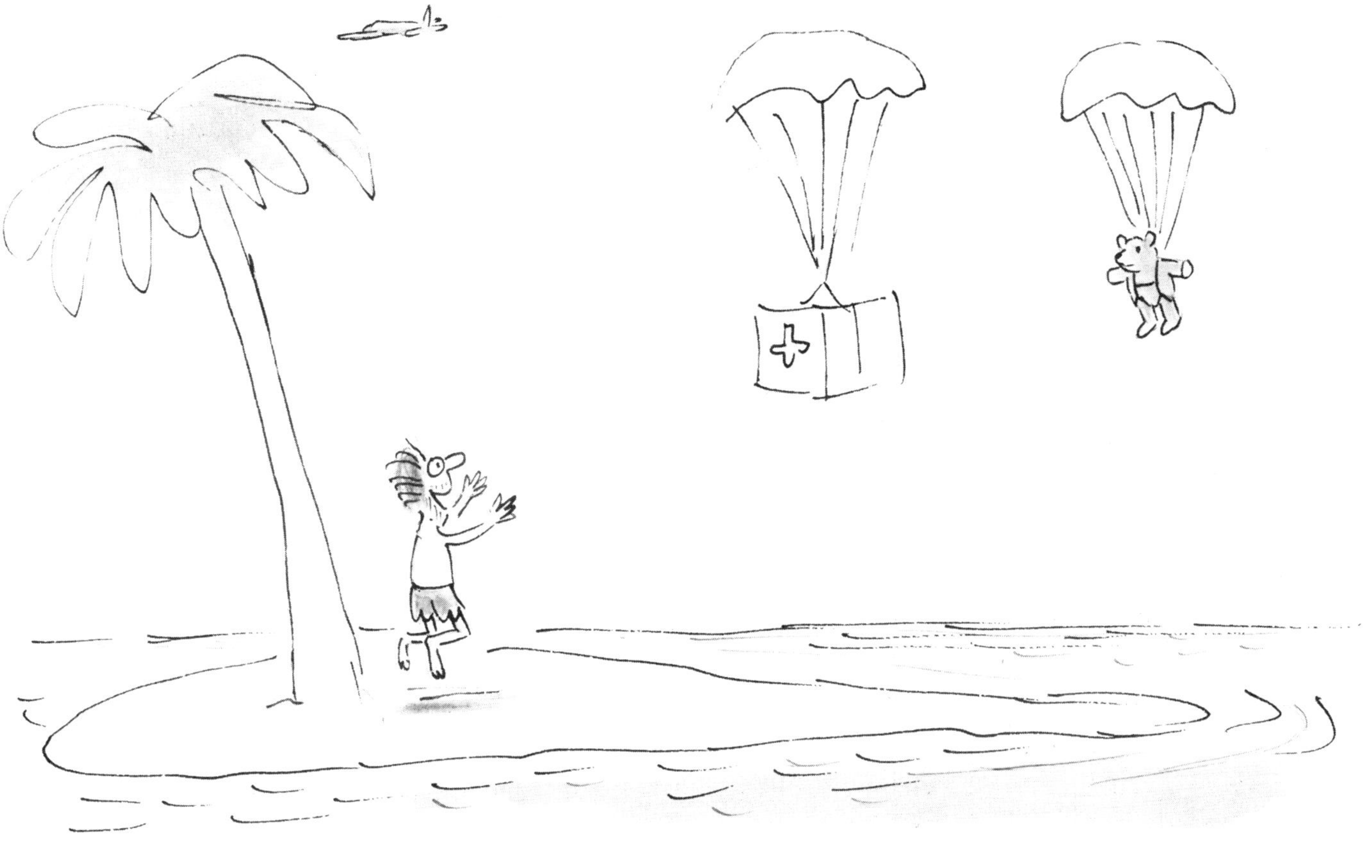

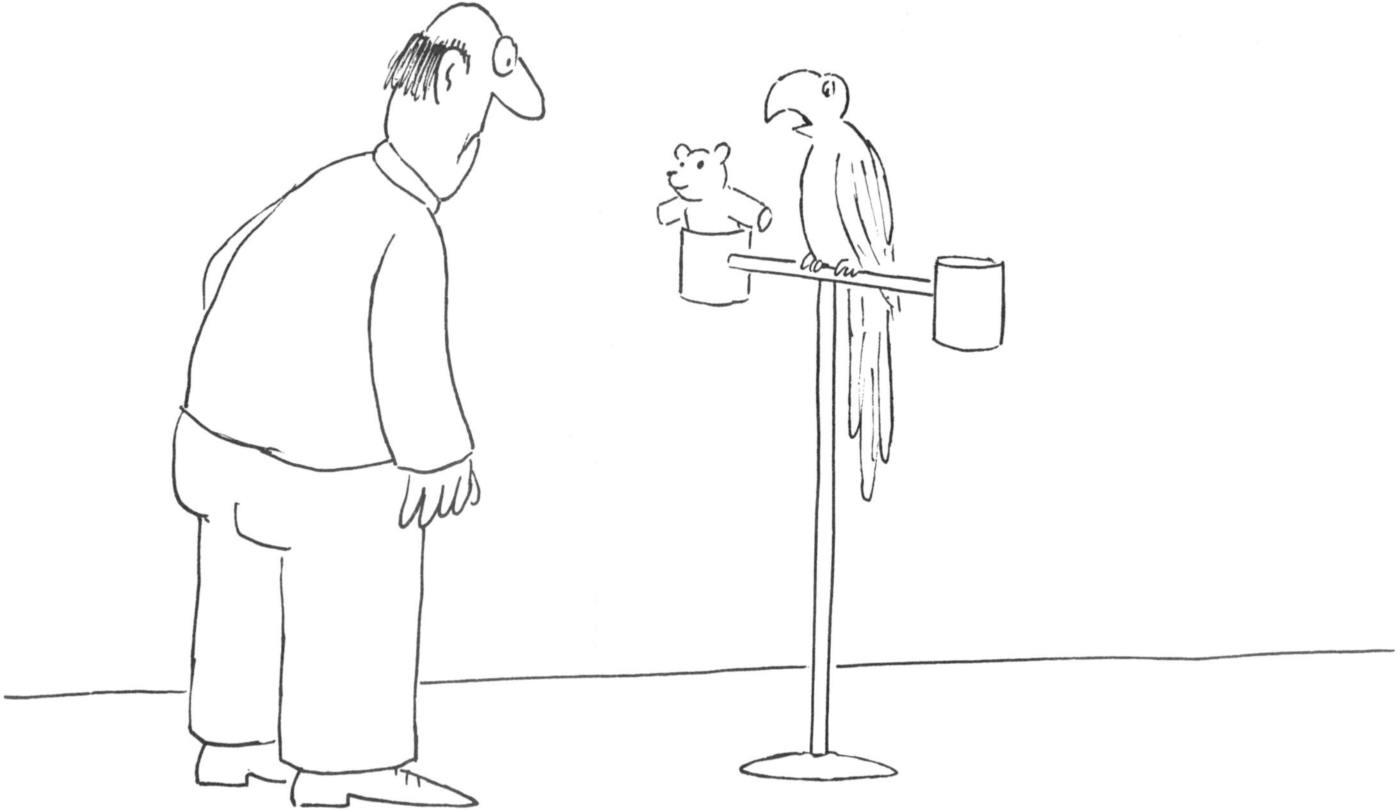

"George wants a cracker too."

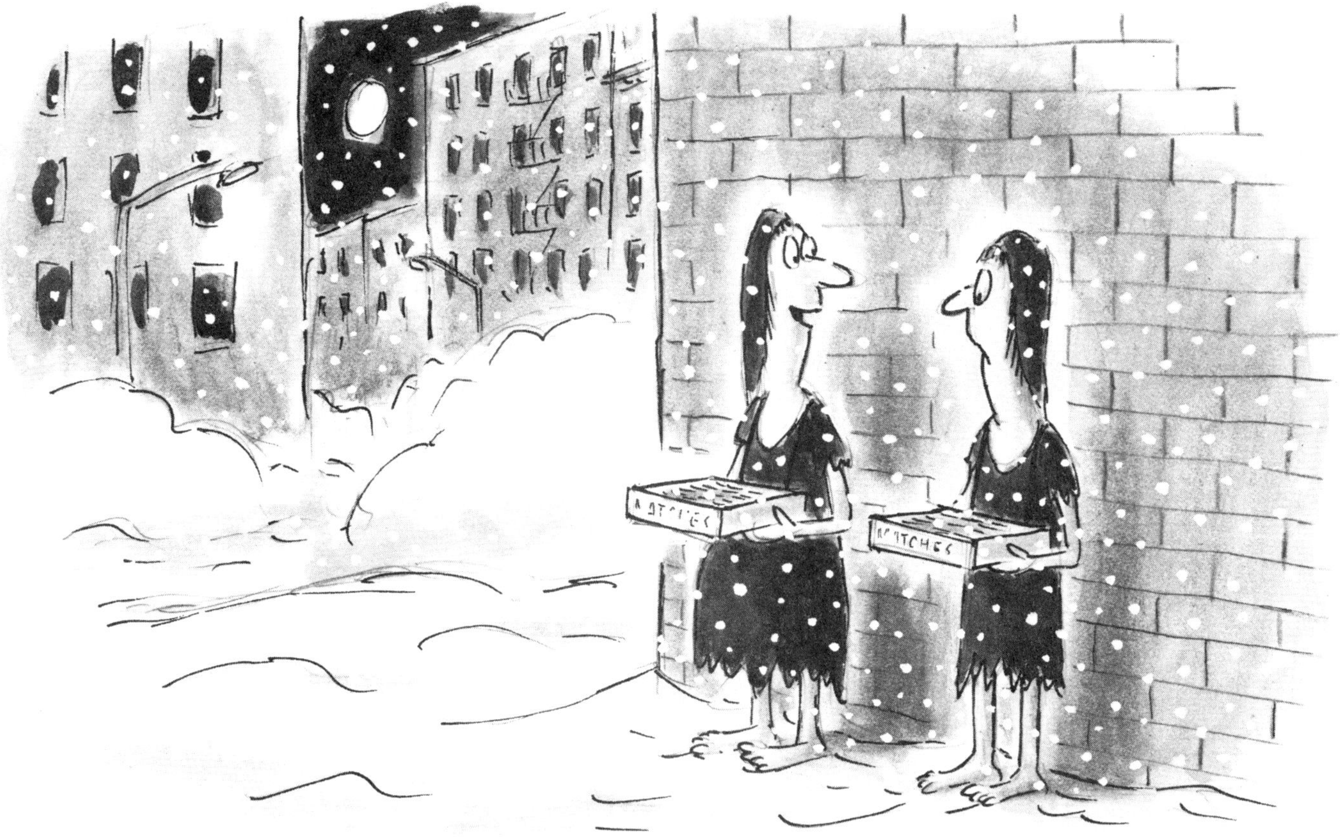

"No, I'm not pregnant. I have my teddy bear down there keeping me warm."

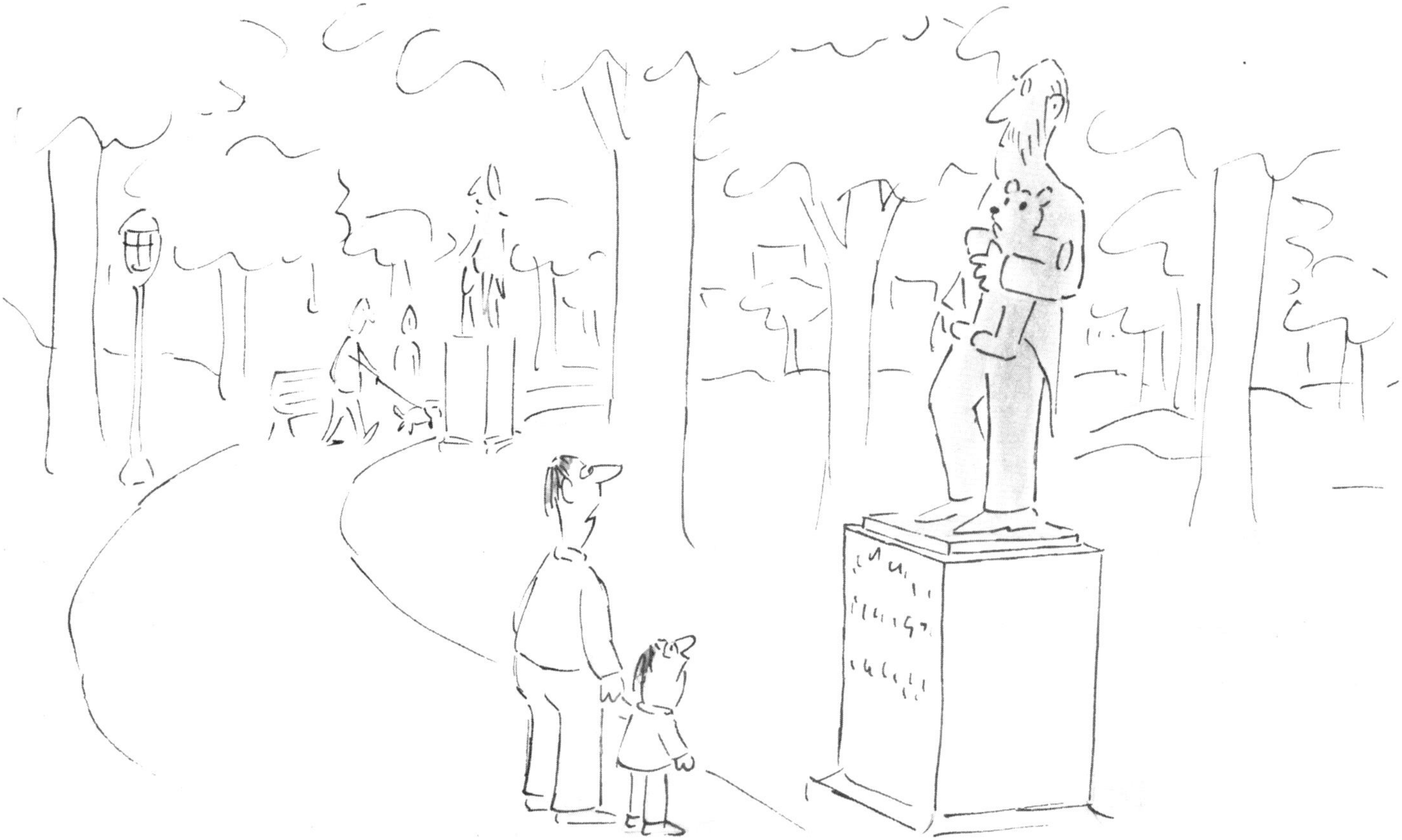

"There are no great men, my son. Just great teddy bears."

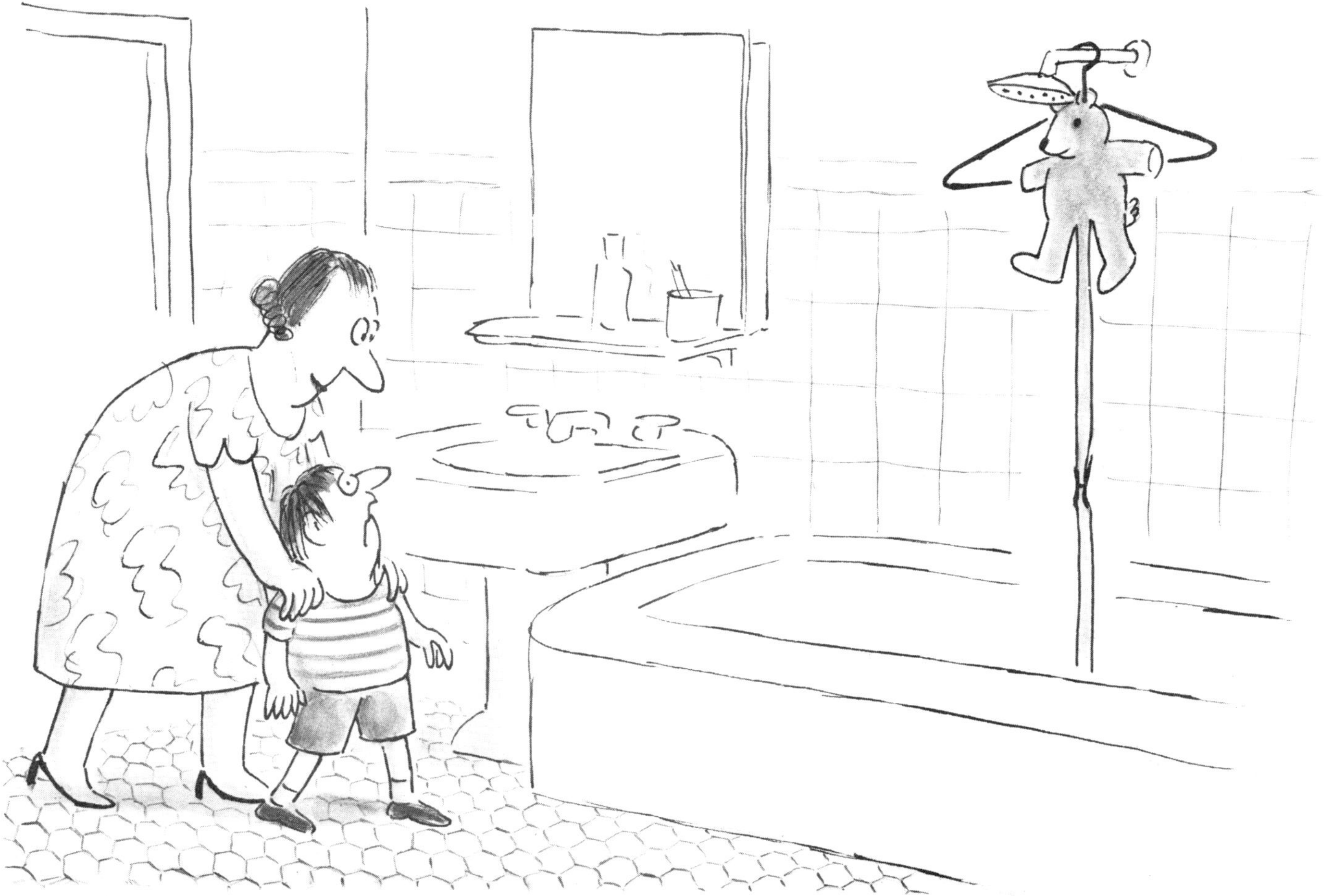

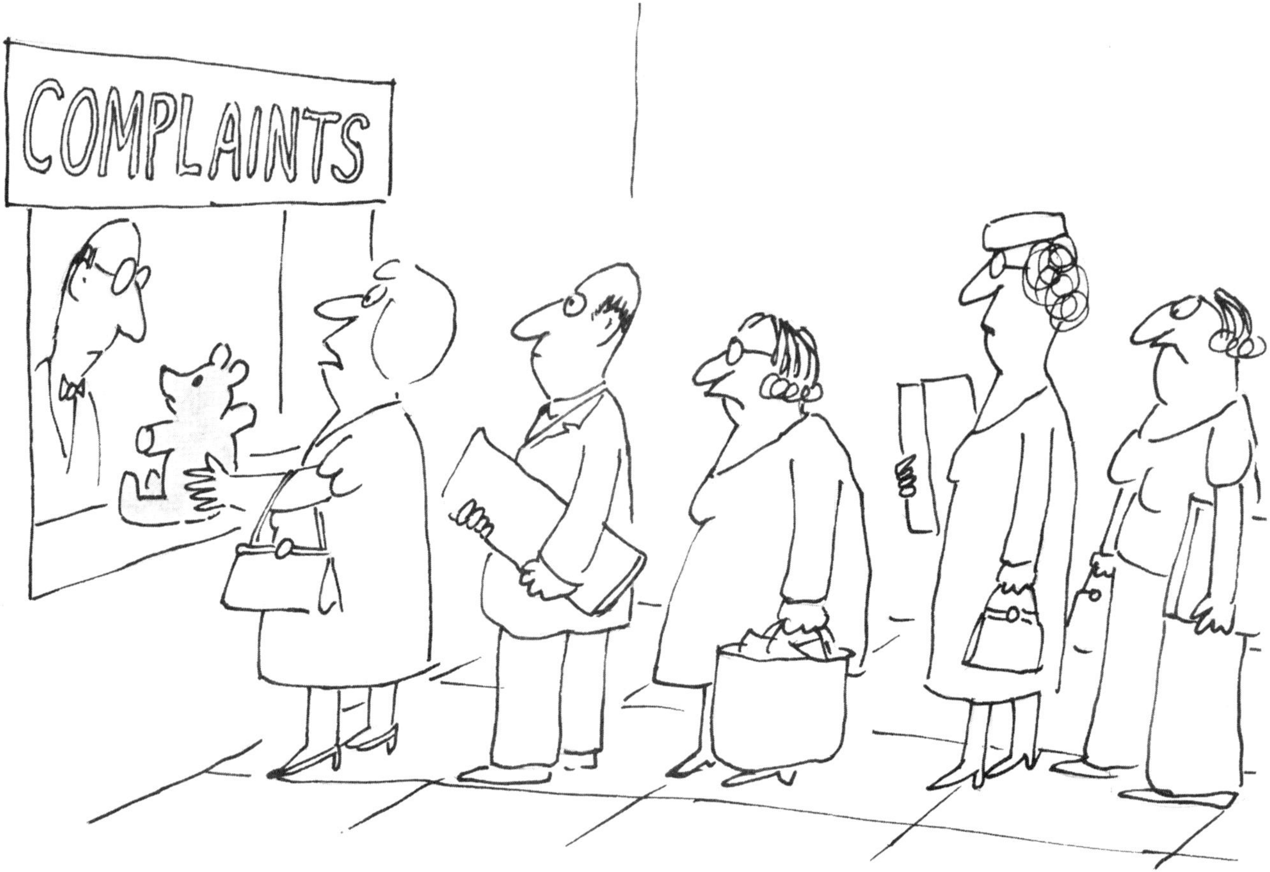
COMPLAINTS

"He's aloof."

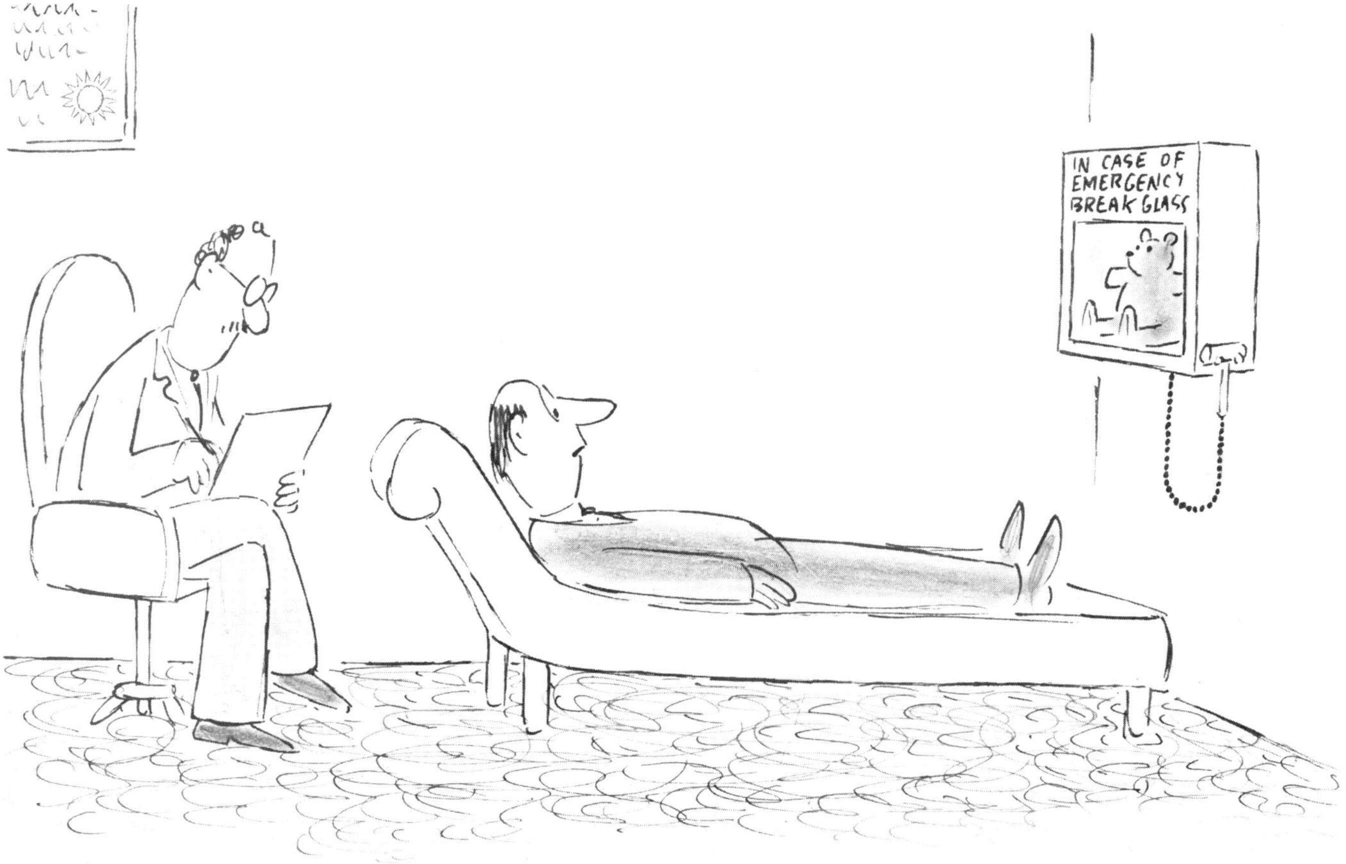
IN CASE OF
EMERGENCY
BREAK GLASS

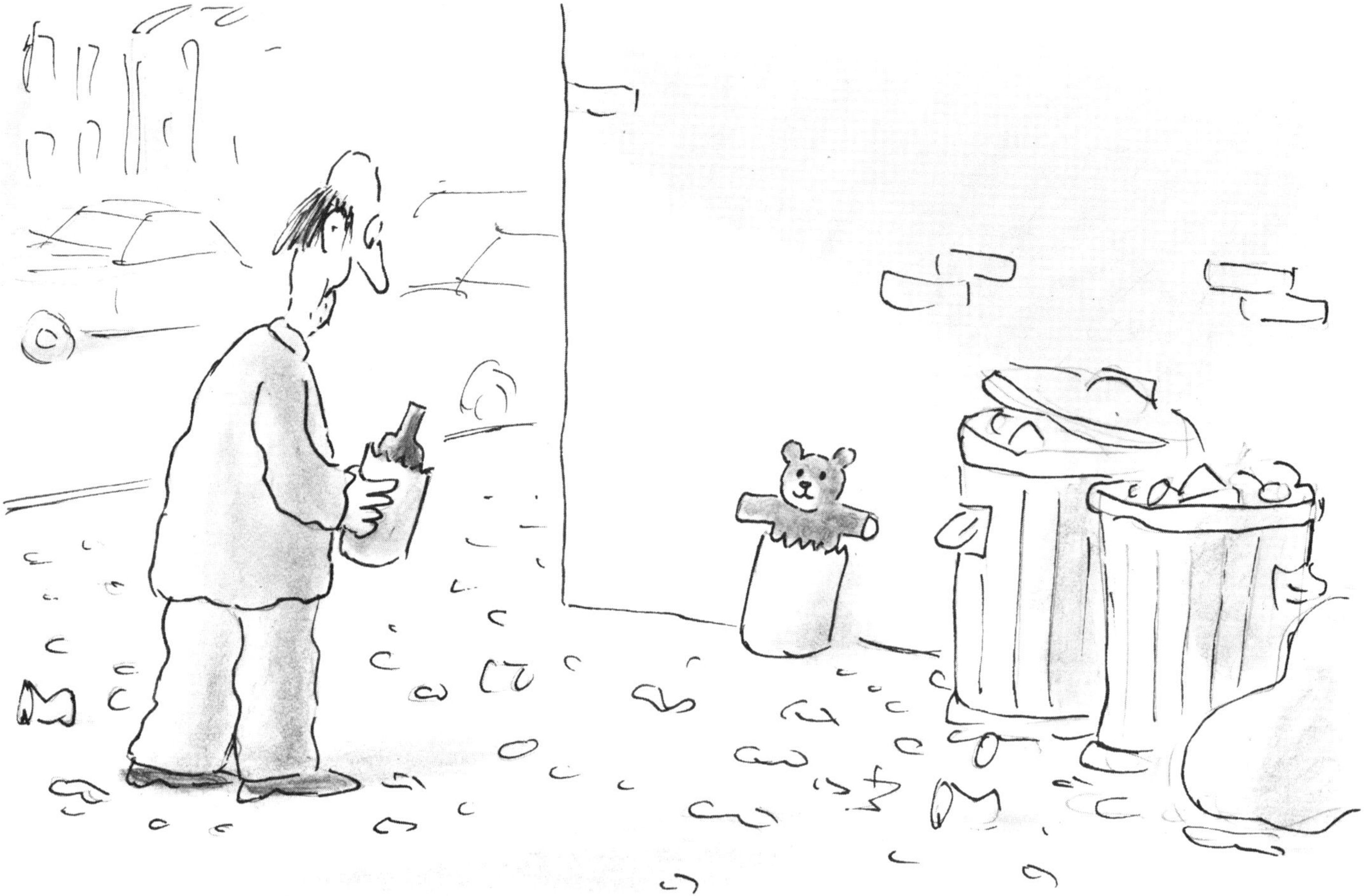

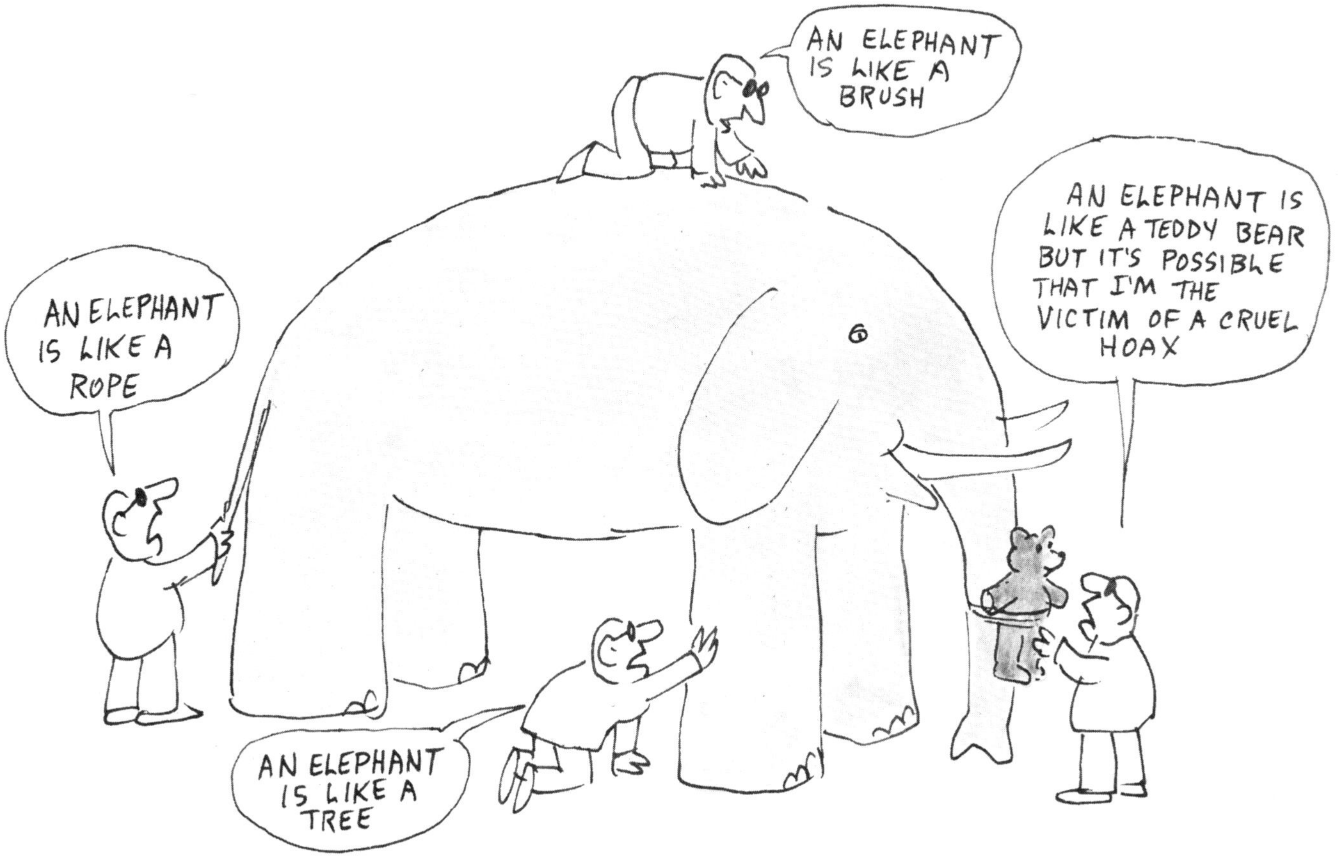
AN ELEPHANT IS LIKE A BRUSH
AN ELEPHANT IS LIKE A ROPE
AN ELEPHANT IS LIKE A TEDDY BEAR BUT IT'S POSSIBLE THAT I'M THE VICTIM OF A CRUEL HOAX
AN ELEPHANT IS LIKE A TREE

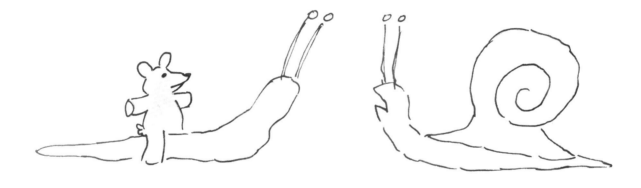

"Frankly, I prefer the security of a shell."

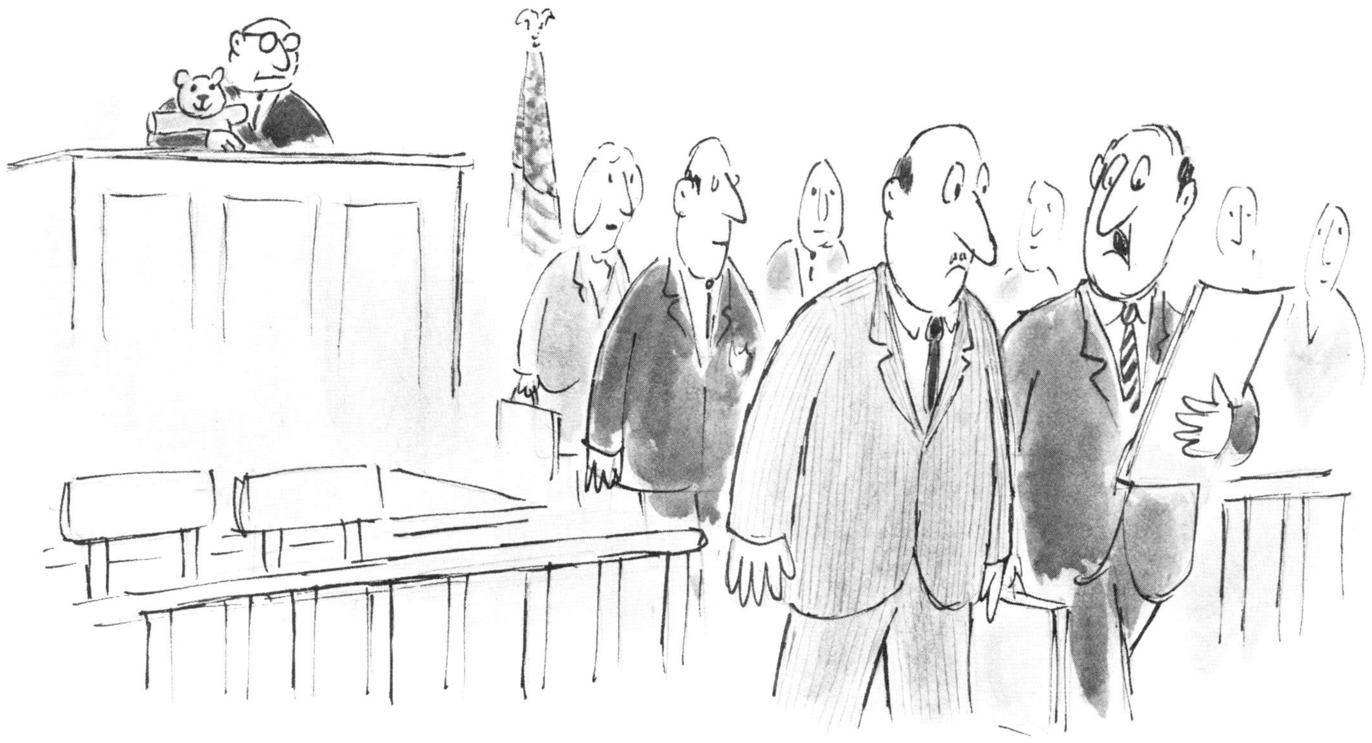

"Don't you worry. I can guarantee that any decision handed down by Judge Roscoe T. Hamber with a concurring opinion by Fluffy will definitely be overturned on appeal."

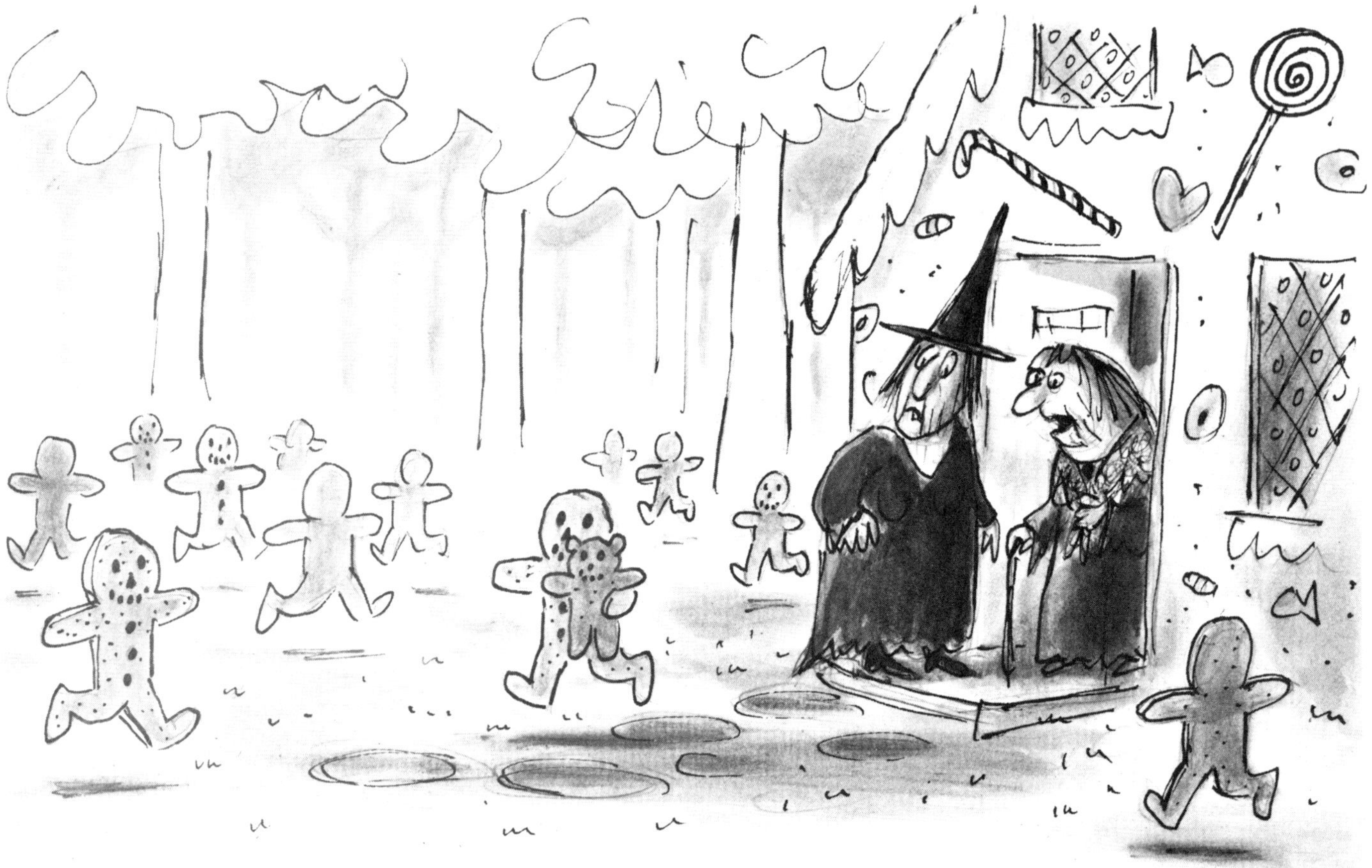

"Every so often I get one who refuses to give up his Teddy Bear."

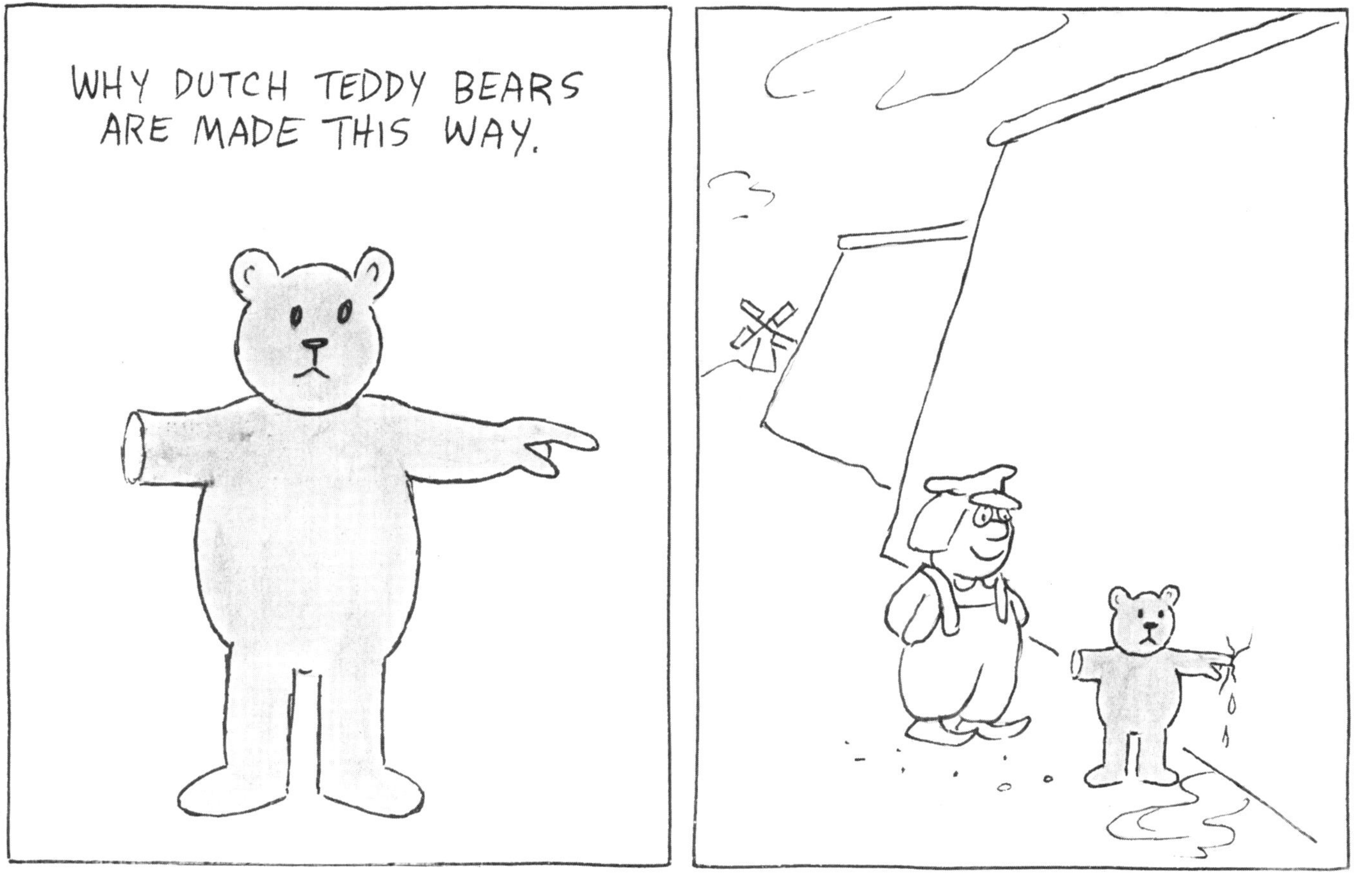
WHY DUTCH TEDDY BEARS
ARE MADE THIS WAY.

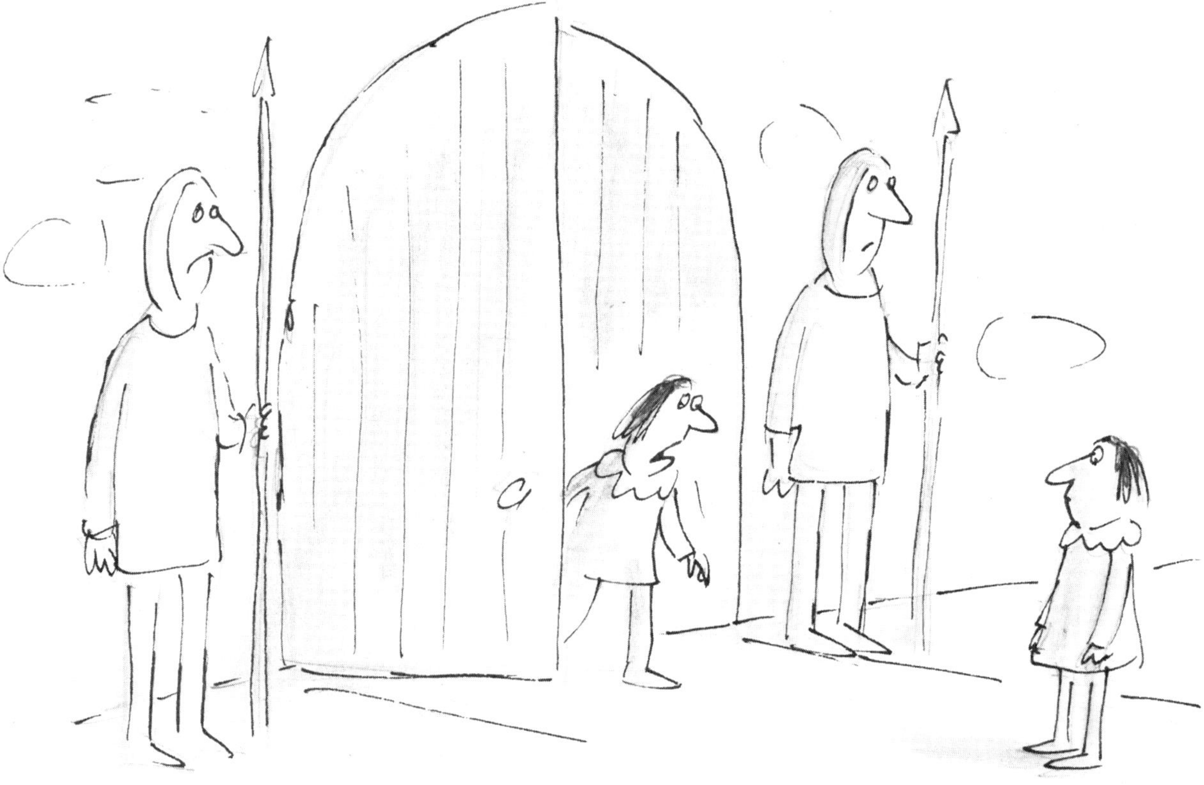

"Lord, what a day! First his pipe. Then his bowl. Then his fiddlers three. . . . And now he wants his goddamn teddy bear."

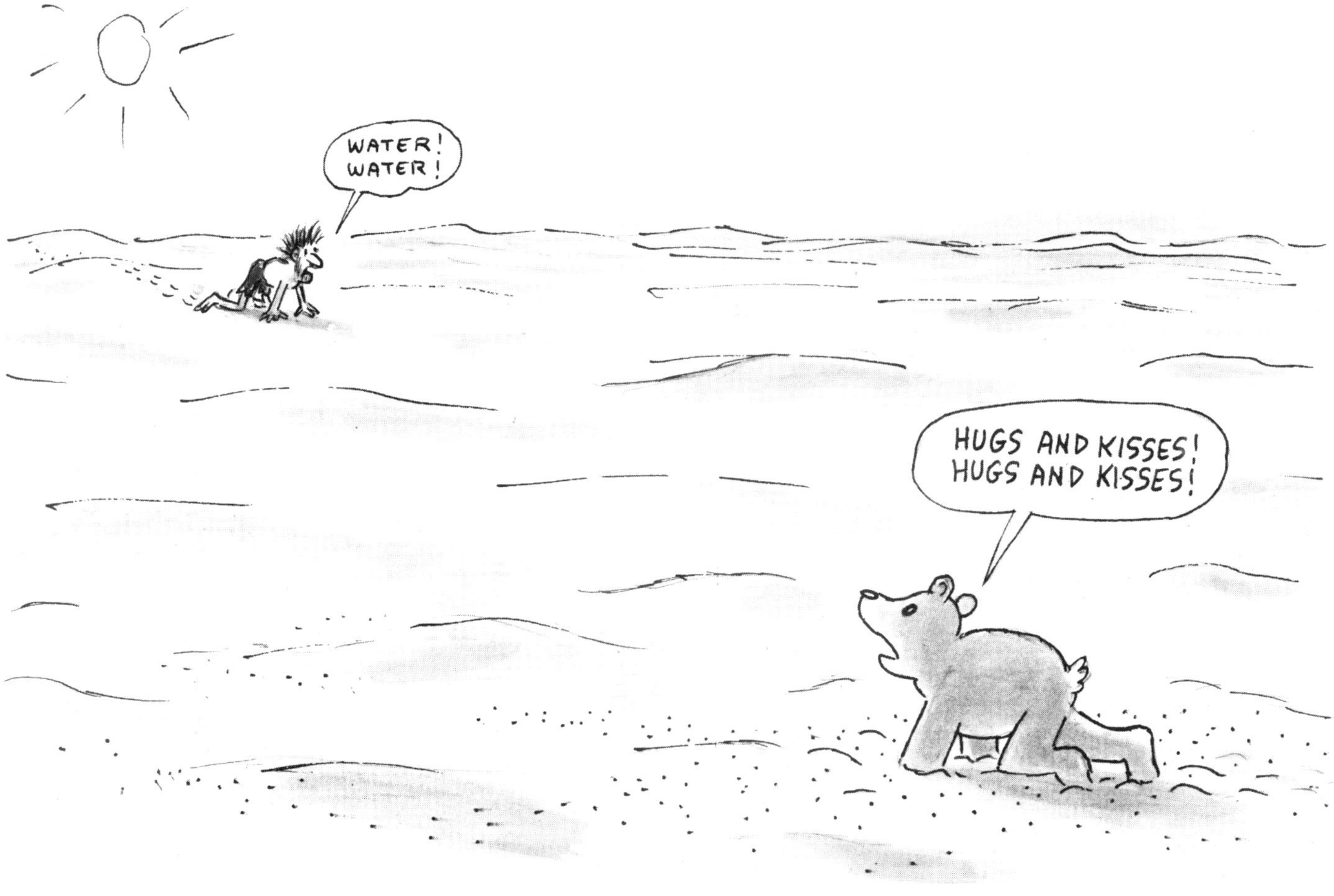
WATER! WATER!
HUGS AND KISSES! HUGS AND KISSES!

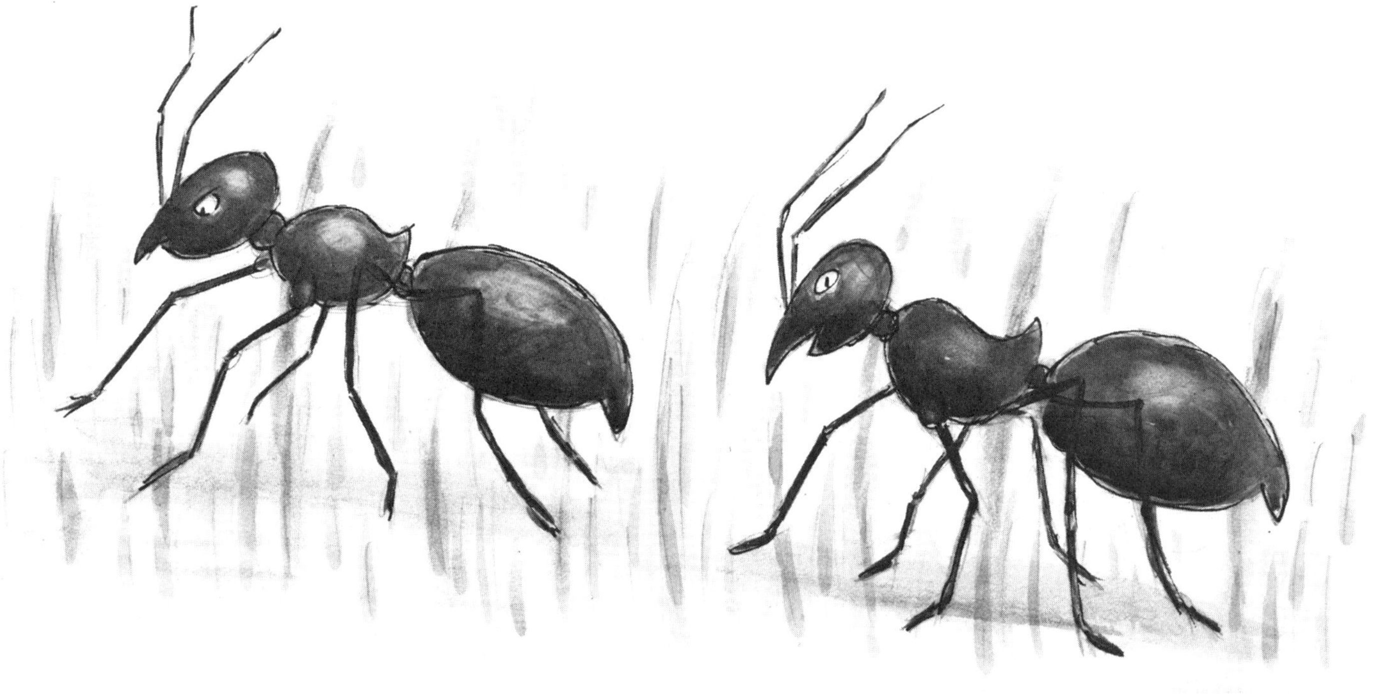

"I know they don't eat and so there's never any food there, but still, what's a teddy bears' picnic without ants?"

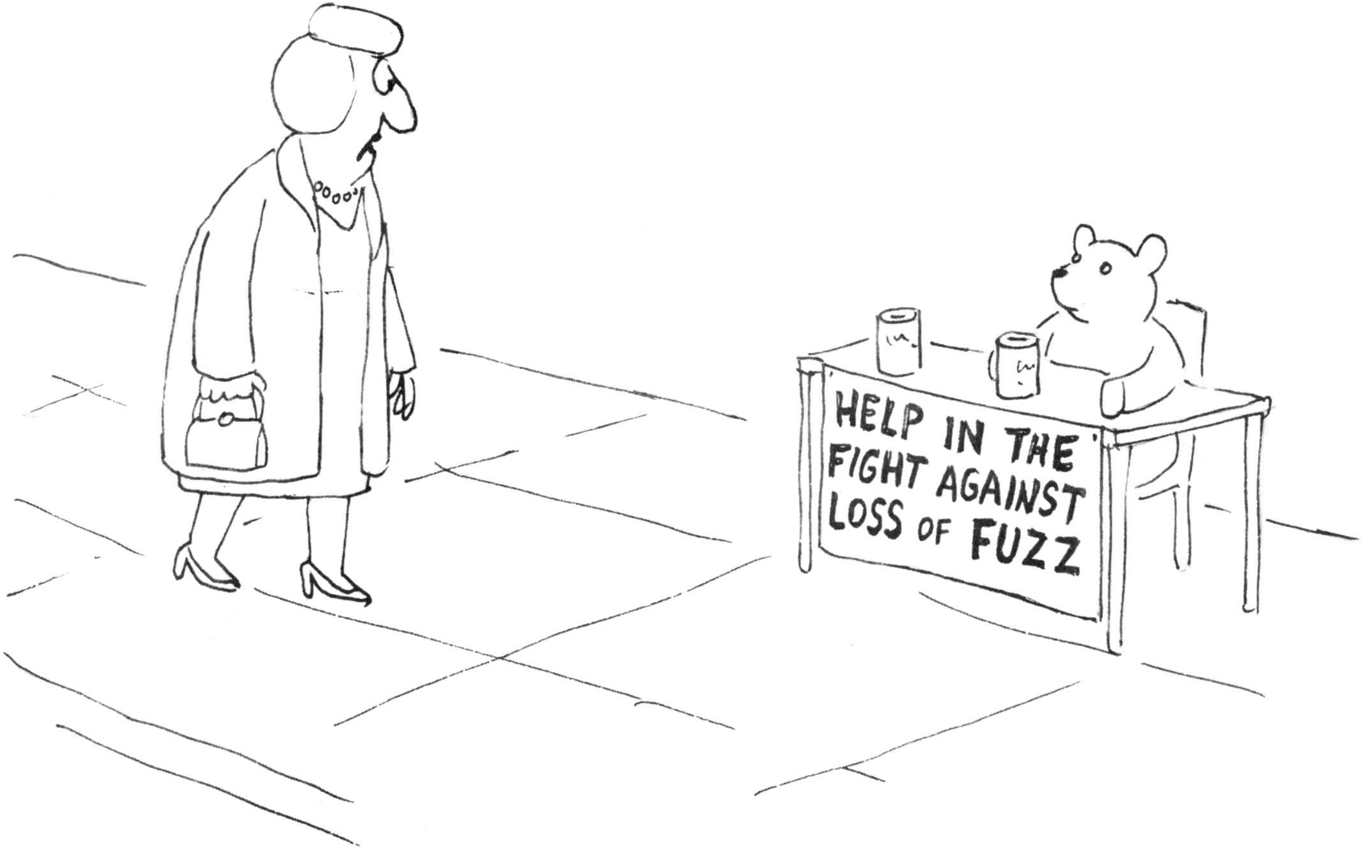
HELP IN THE
FIGHT AGAINST
LOSS OF FUZZ

"Gosh! What a clever way to get to feel their tits."

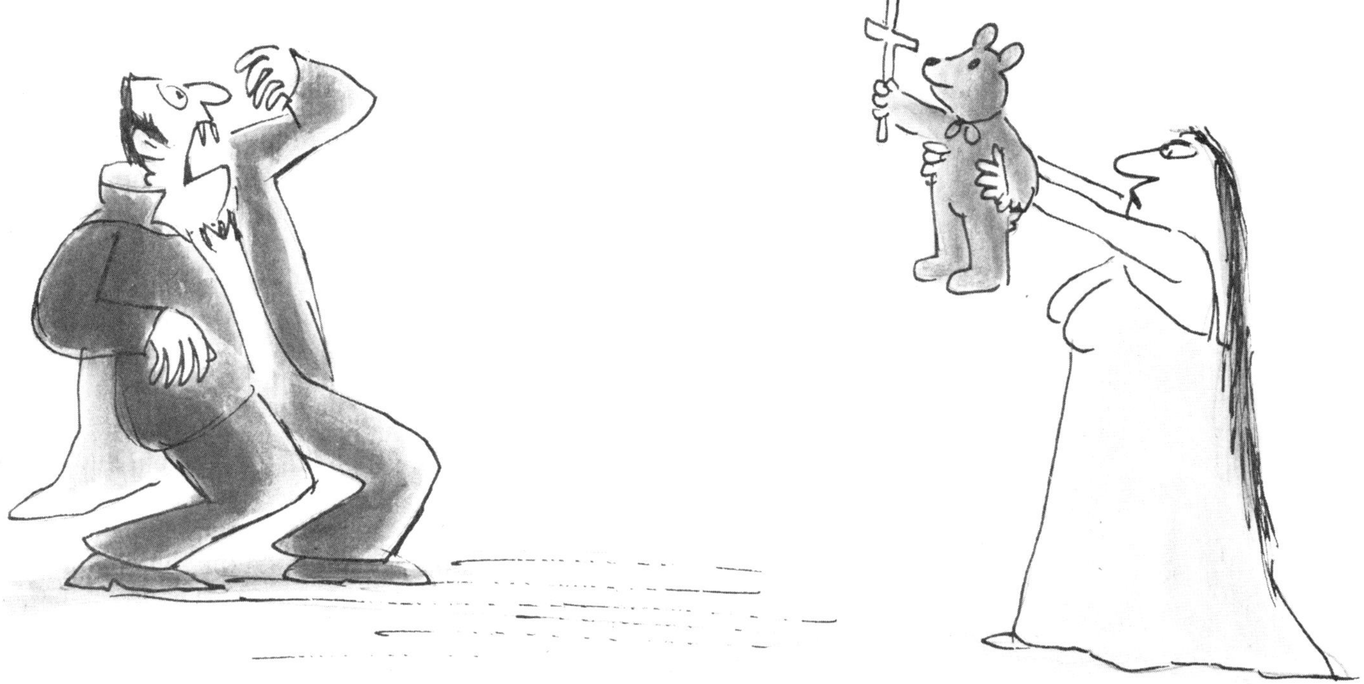

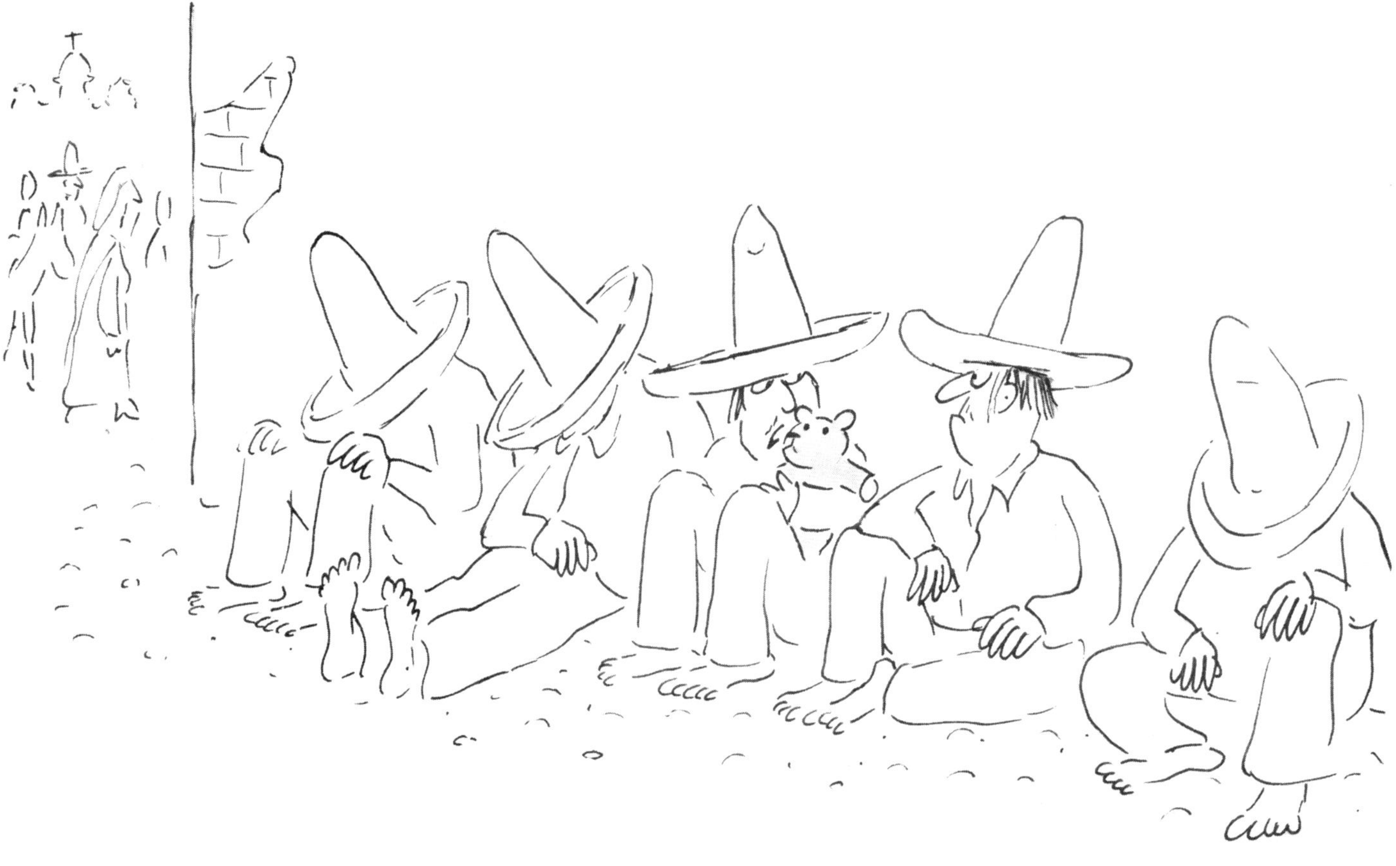

"I know it's not very macho, but I can't go to sleep without him."

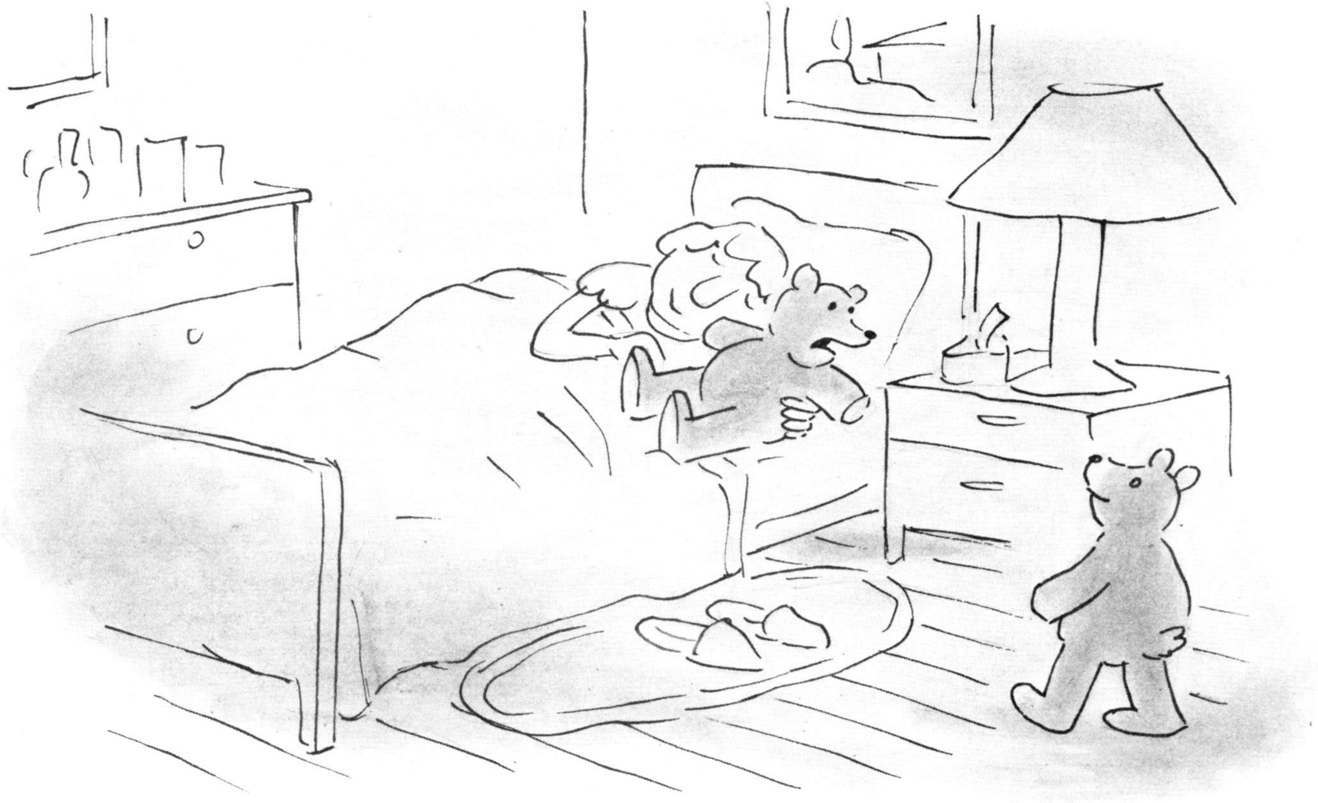

"What happened to you? Your shift was supposed to begin 20 minutes ago."

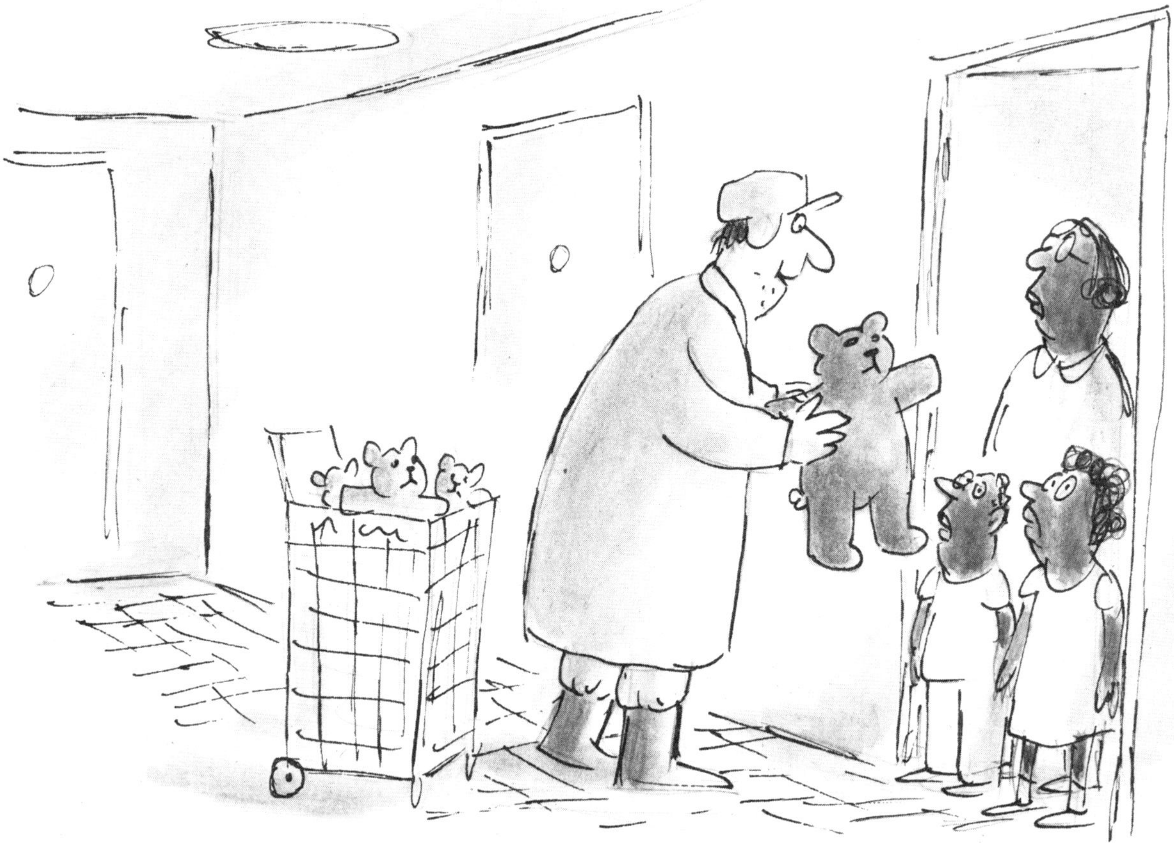

"It's a gift from the landlord. It will keep you warm when there's no heat."

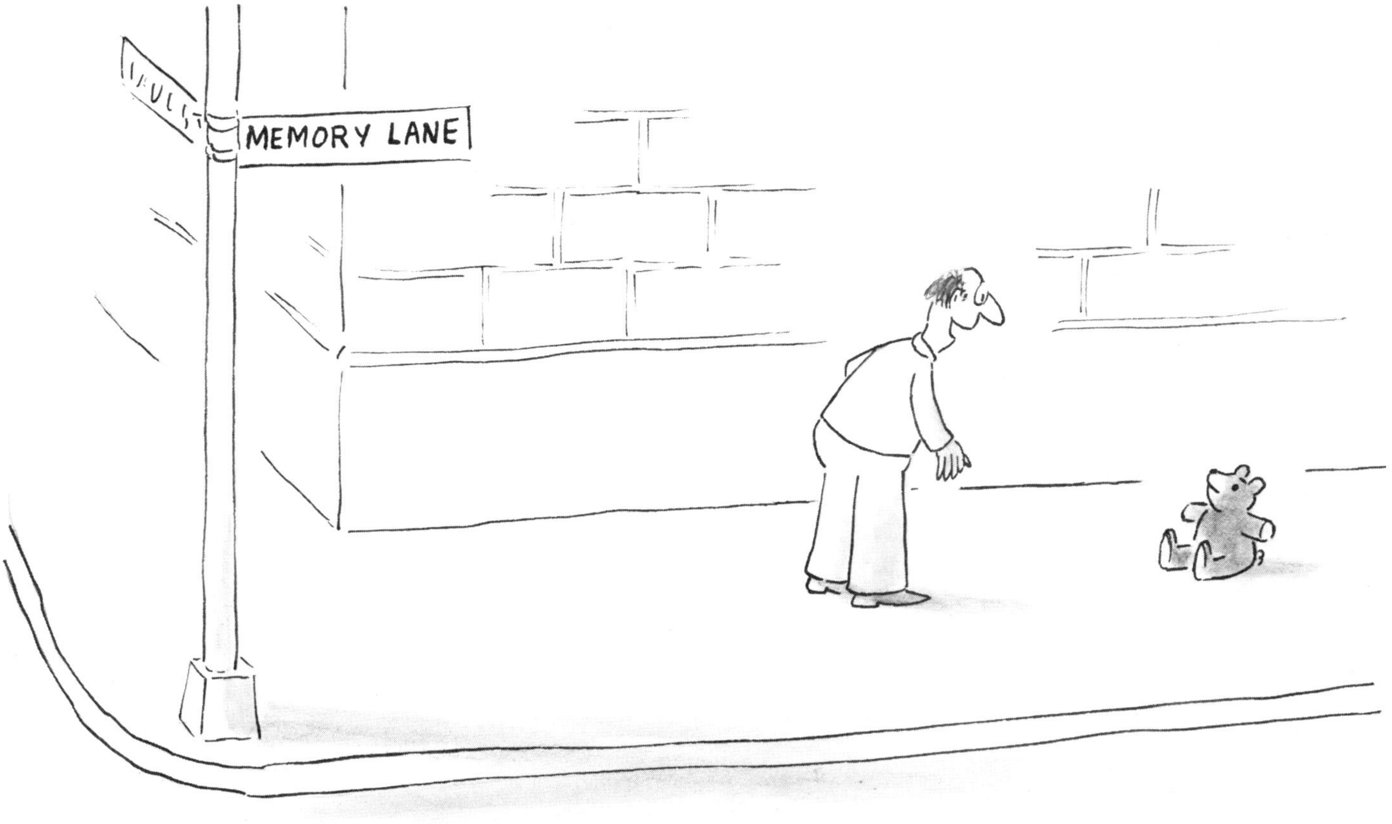
MEMORY LANE

"Why, it's Binkie!"

Lewis Carroll's Teddy Bear

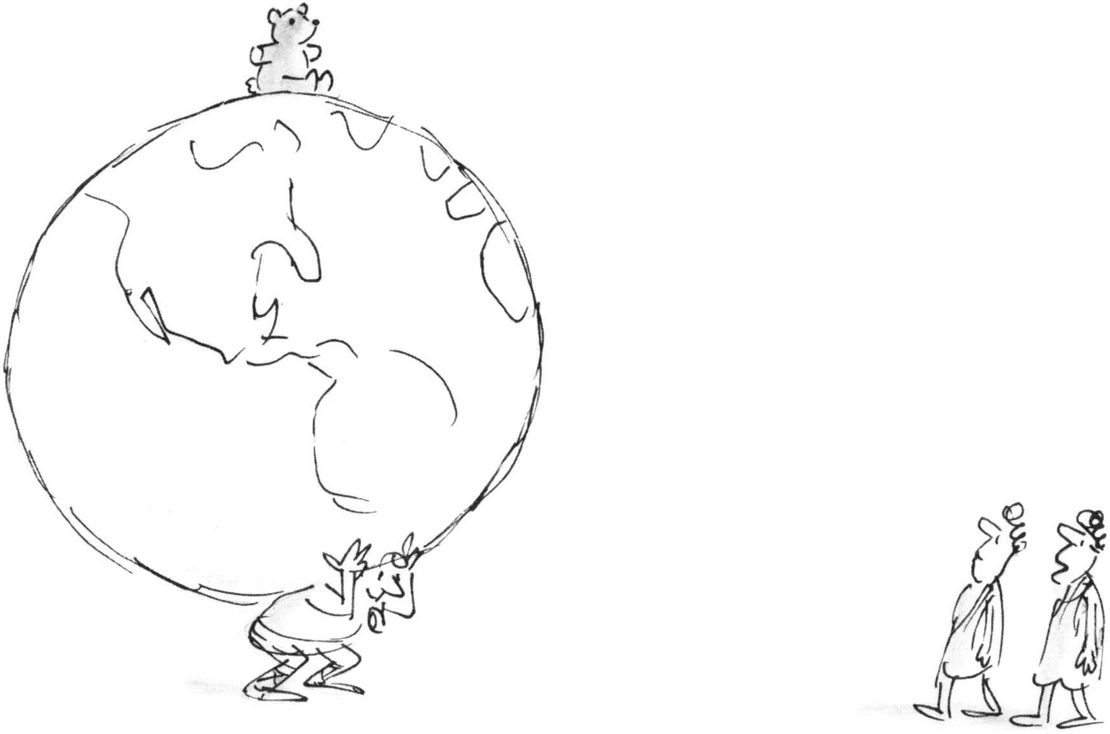

"For once all is right with the world."

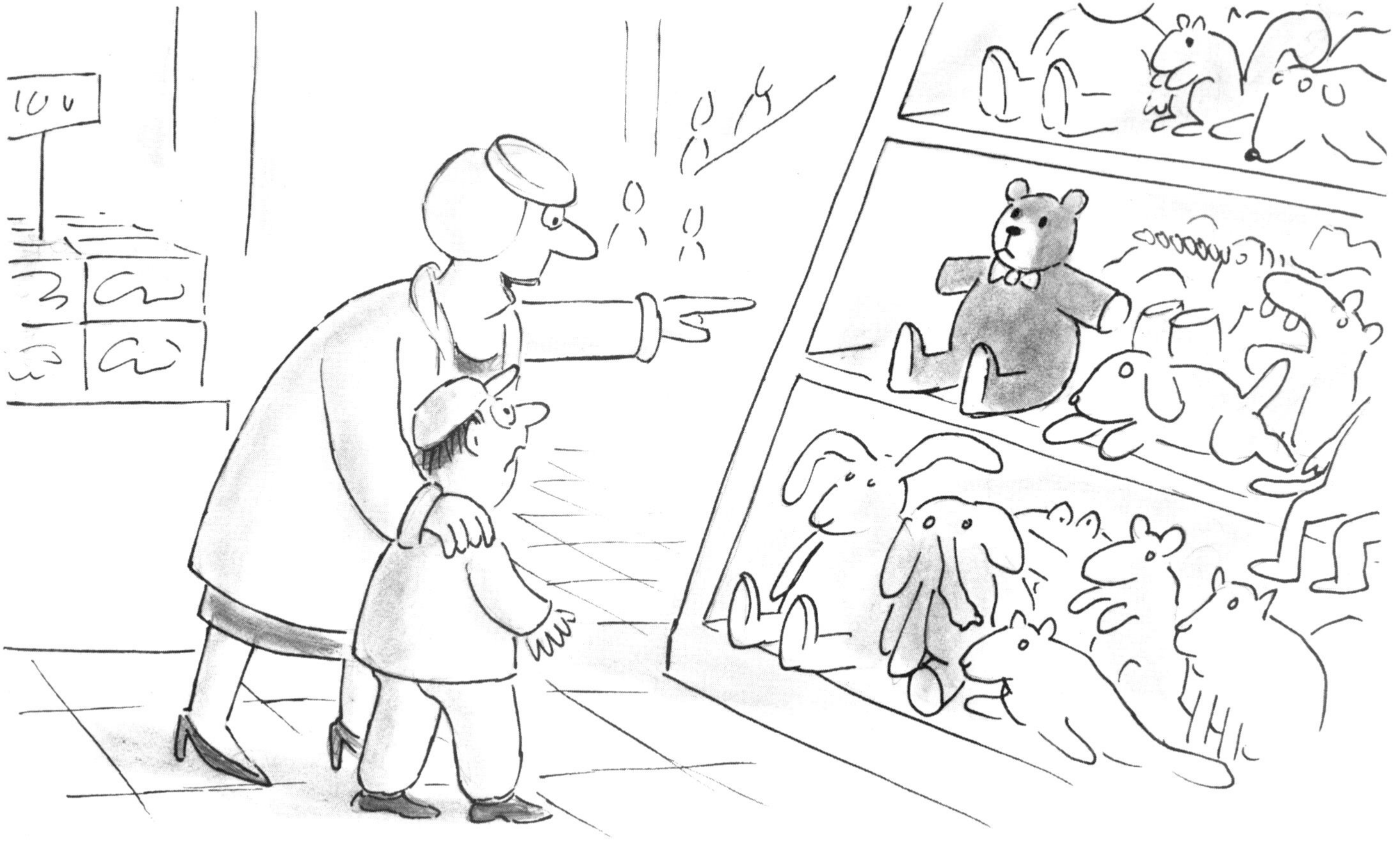

"See what happens to your arms when you play with yourself?"

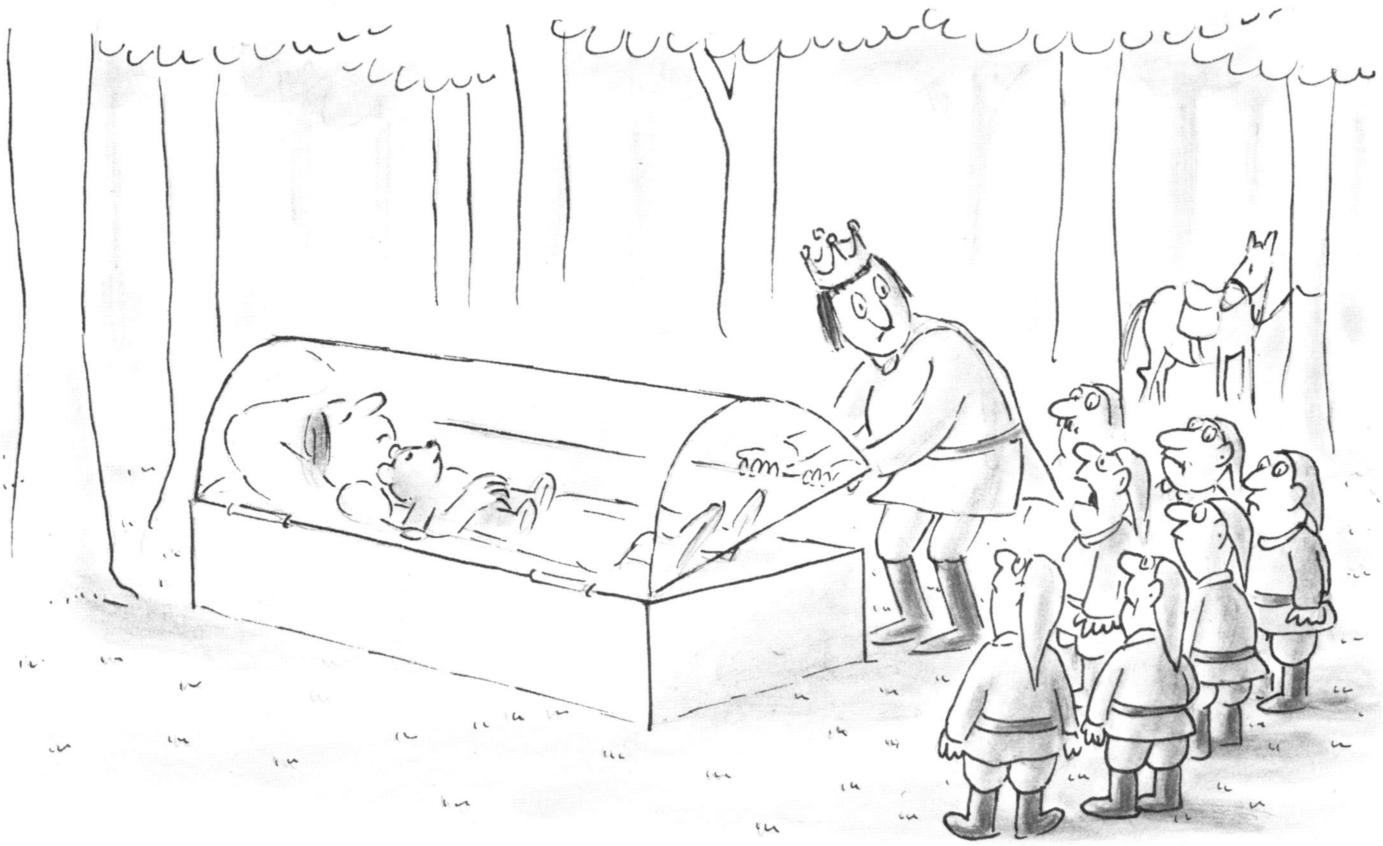

“Don’t forget. The teddy bear belongs to us.”

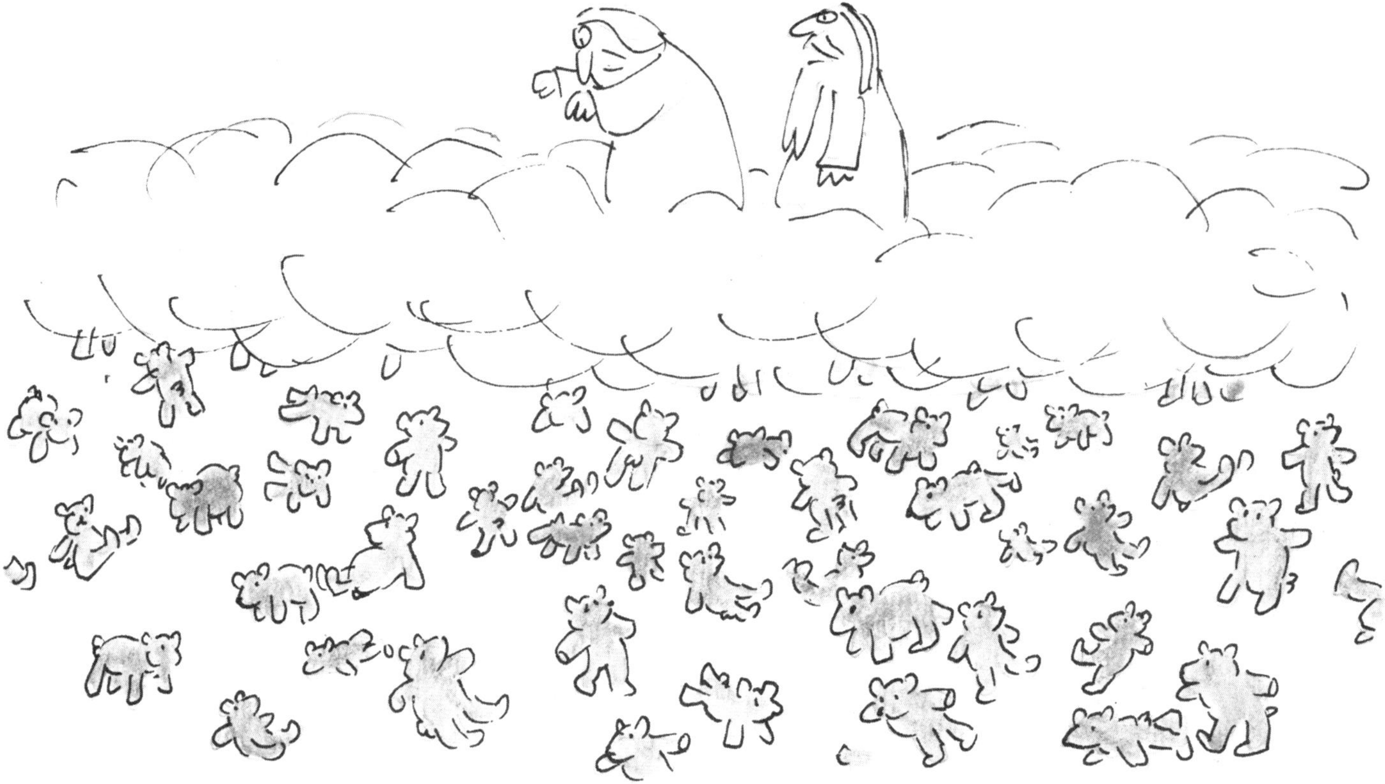

"See? I told you teddy bears don't make a good plague. Now let's go back to frogs."

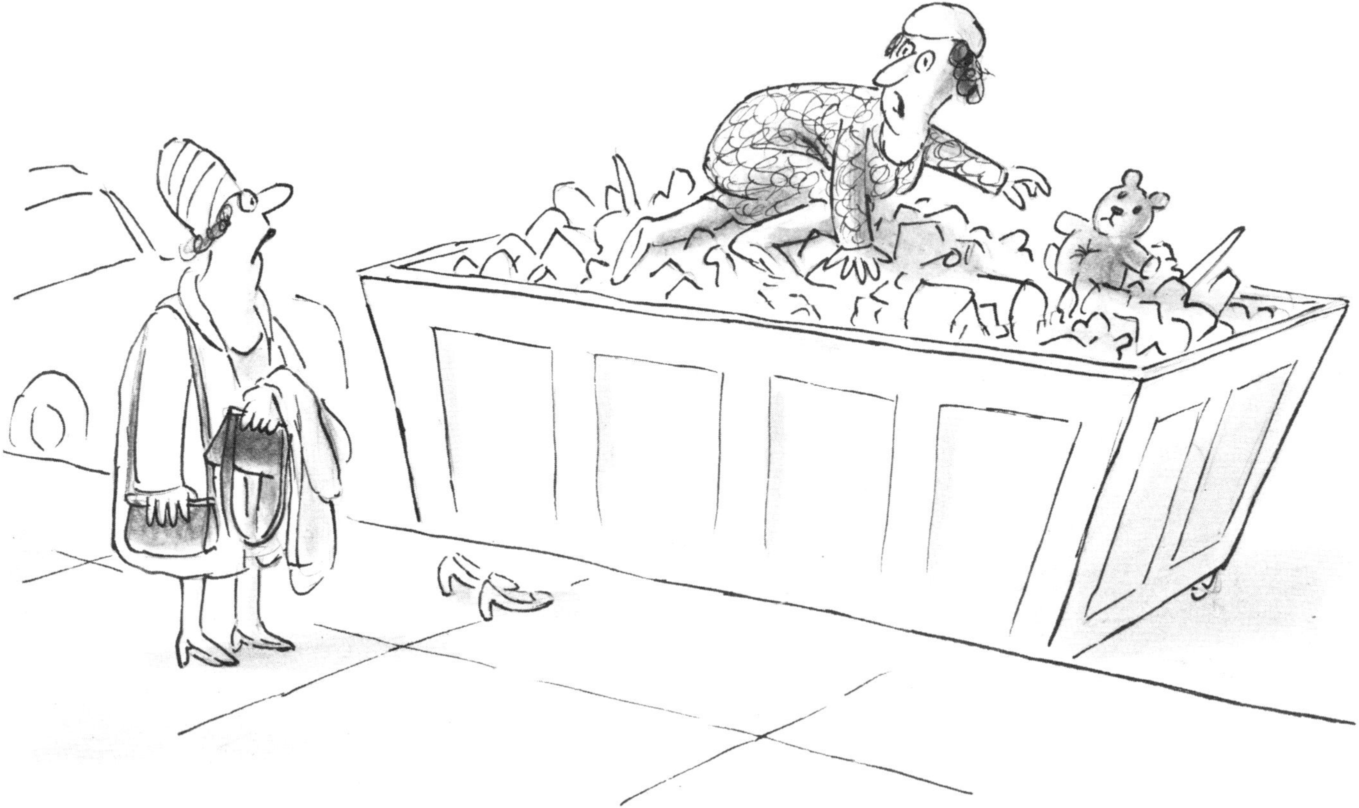

"Ordinarily I never take anything from the garbage, but in this case I have to make an exception."

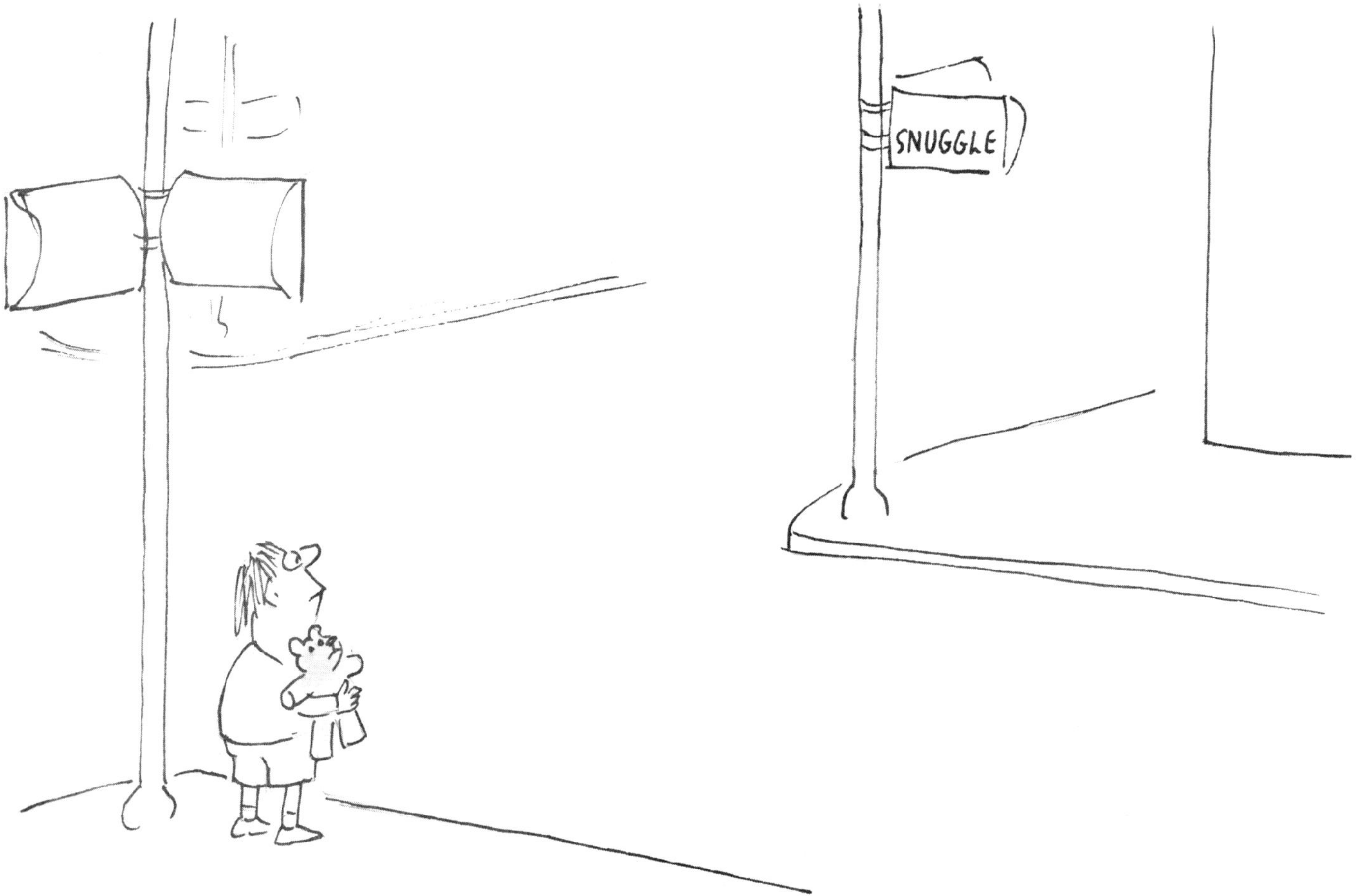
SNUGGLE

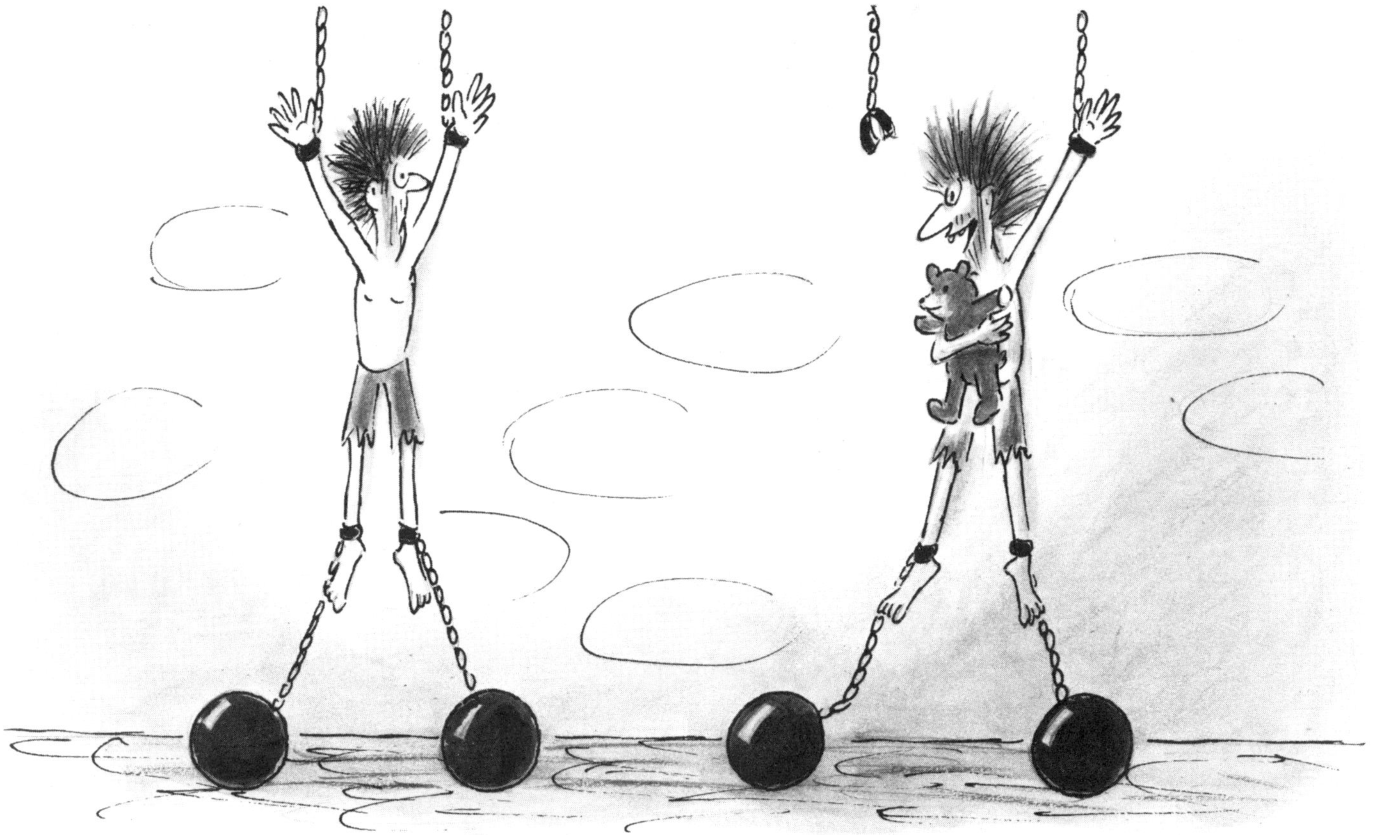

"After ten years they give you certain privileges."

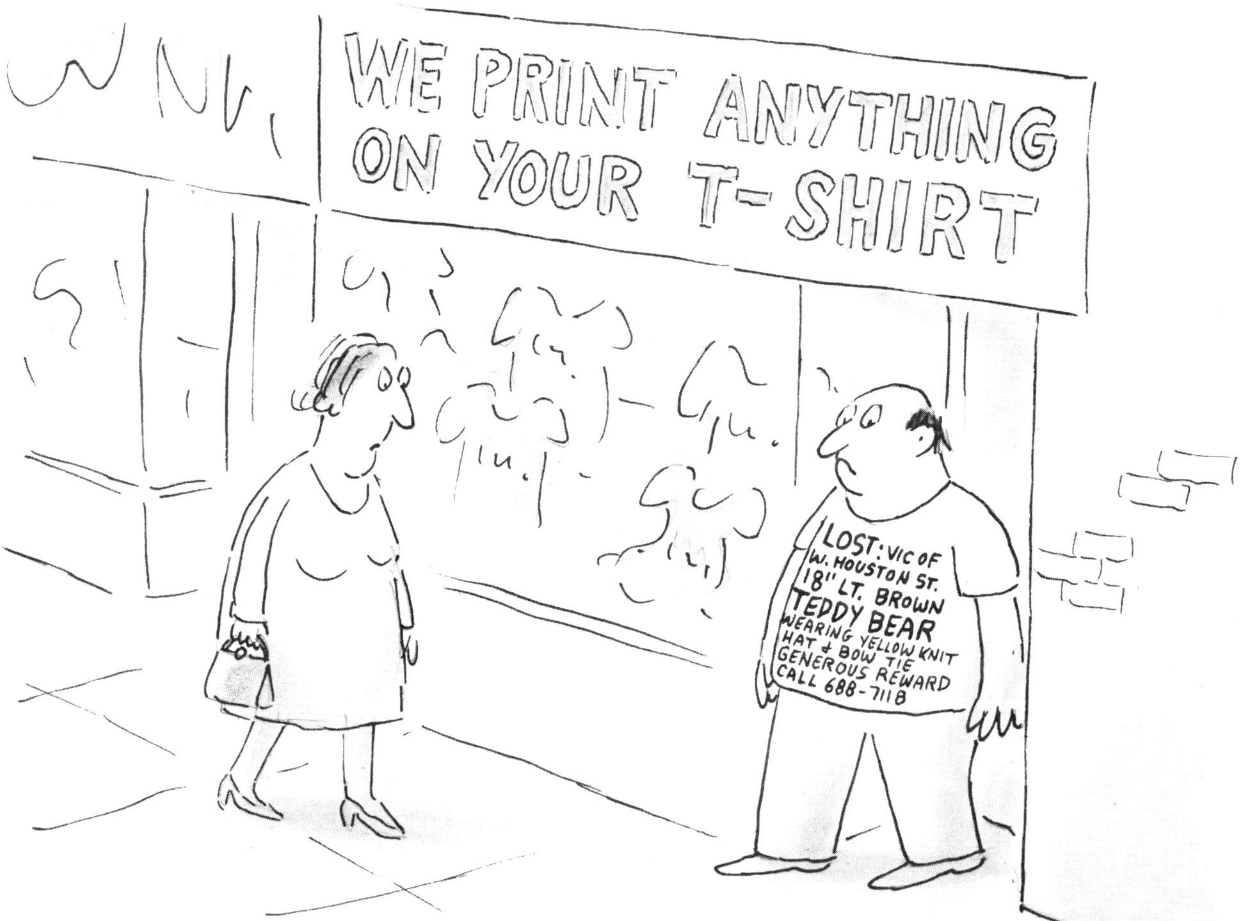
WE PRINT ANYTHING ON YOUR T-SHIRT
LOST: VIC OF W. HOUSTON ST. 18" LT. BROWN TEDDY BEAR WEARING YELLOW KNIT HAT & BOW TIE GENEROUS REWARD CALL 688-7118

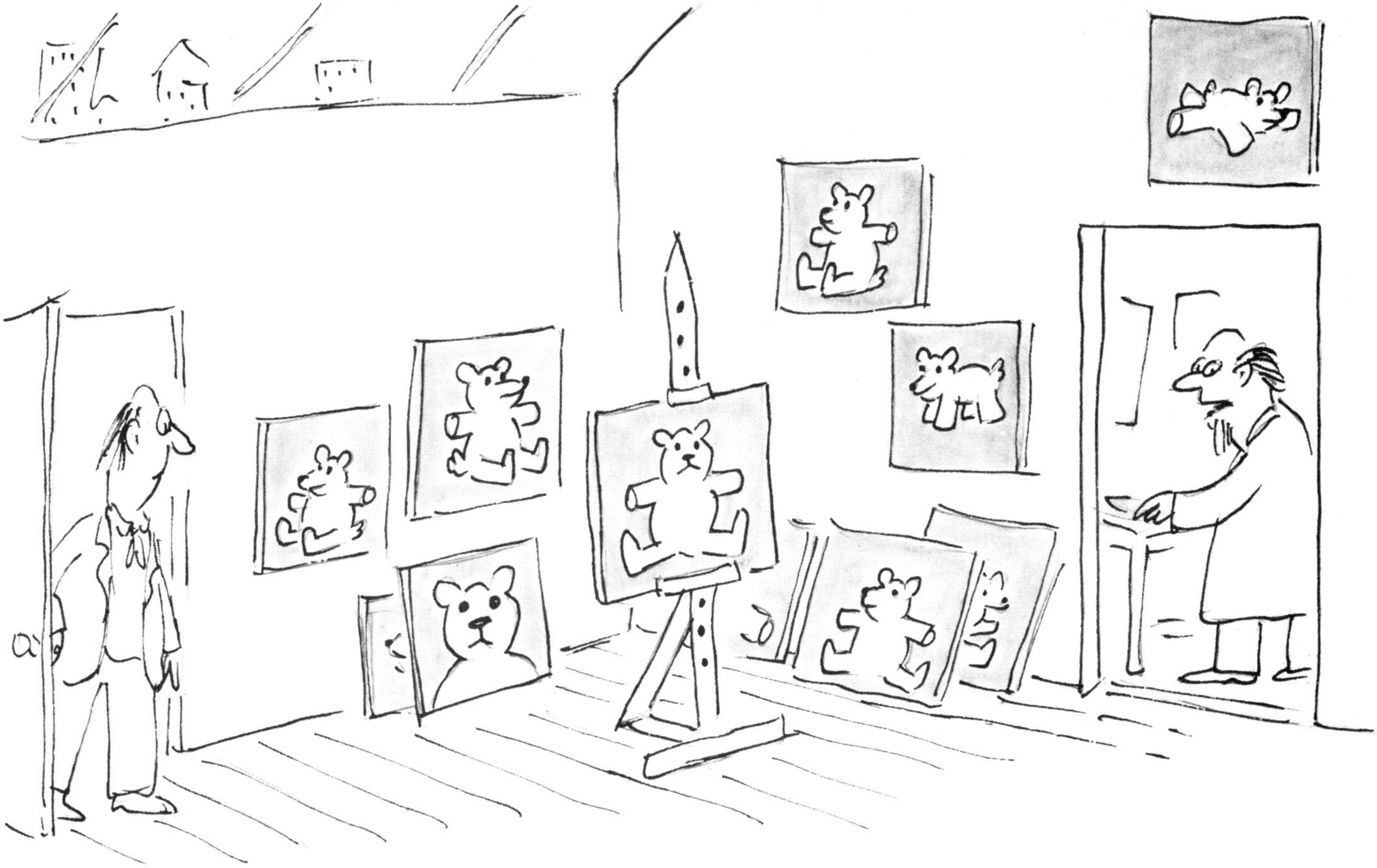

"I'm in here stretching velvet."

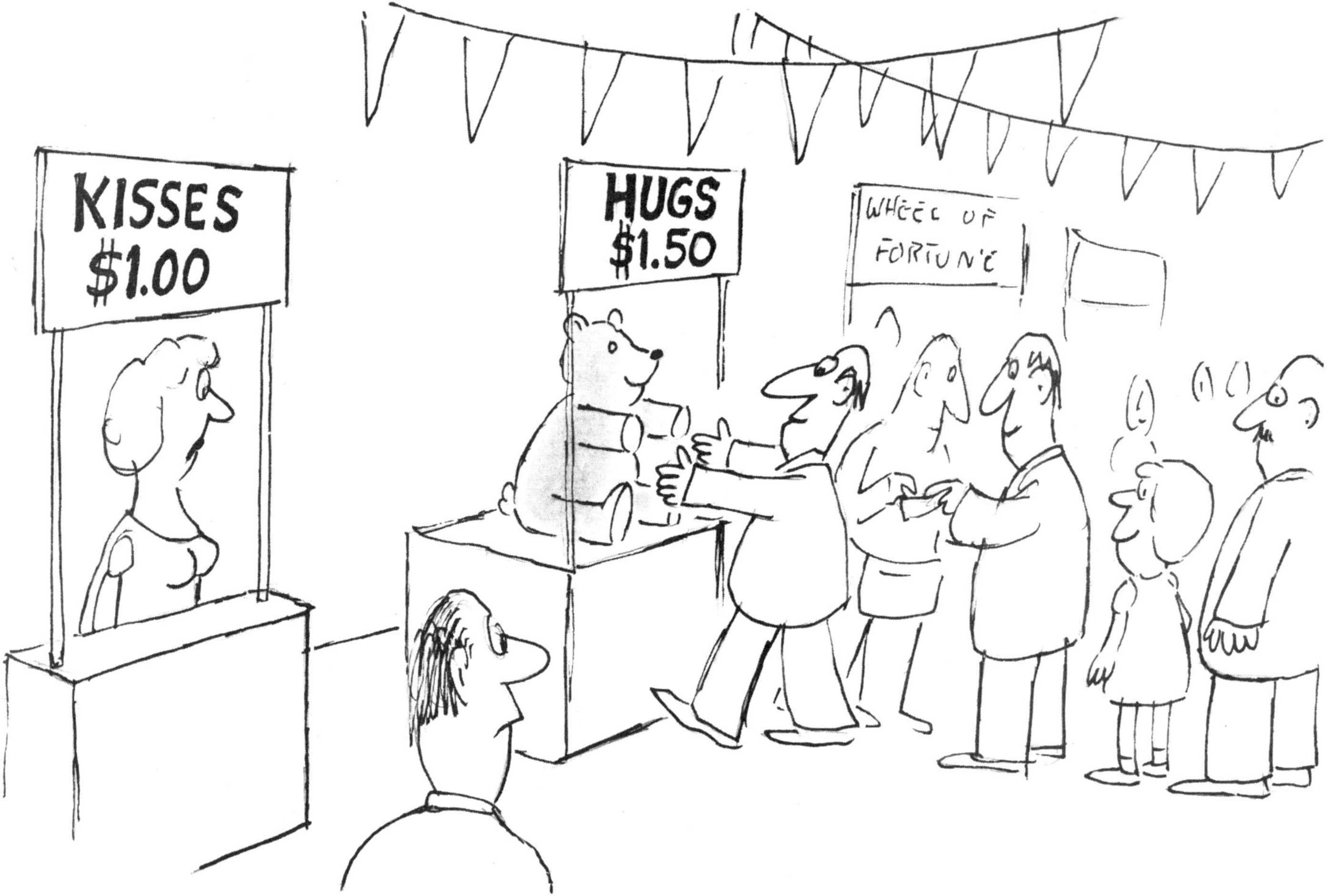
KISSES
$1.00
HUGS
$1.50
WHEEL OF
FORTUNE

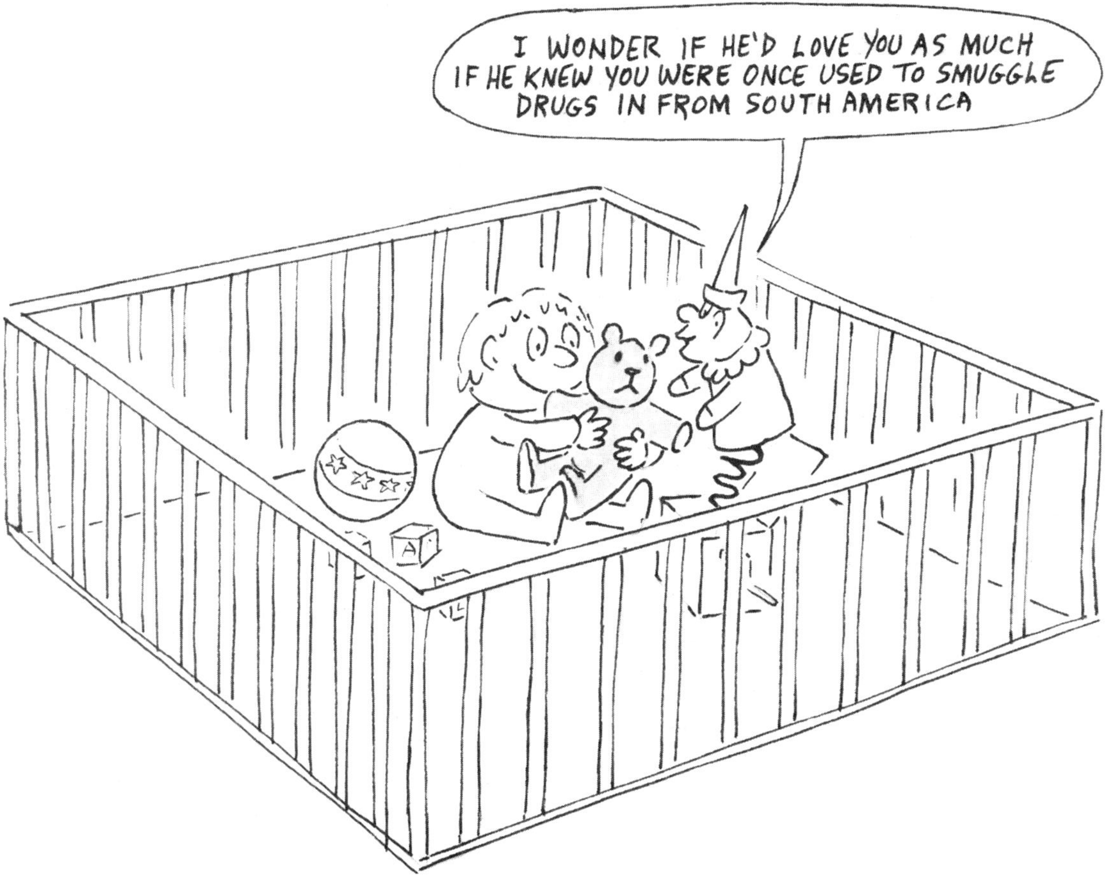
I WONDER IF HE'D LOVE YOU AS MUCH IF HE KNEW YOU WERE ONCE USED TO SMUGGLE DRUGS IN FROM SOUTH AMERICA

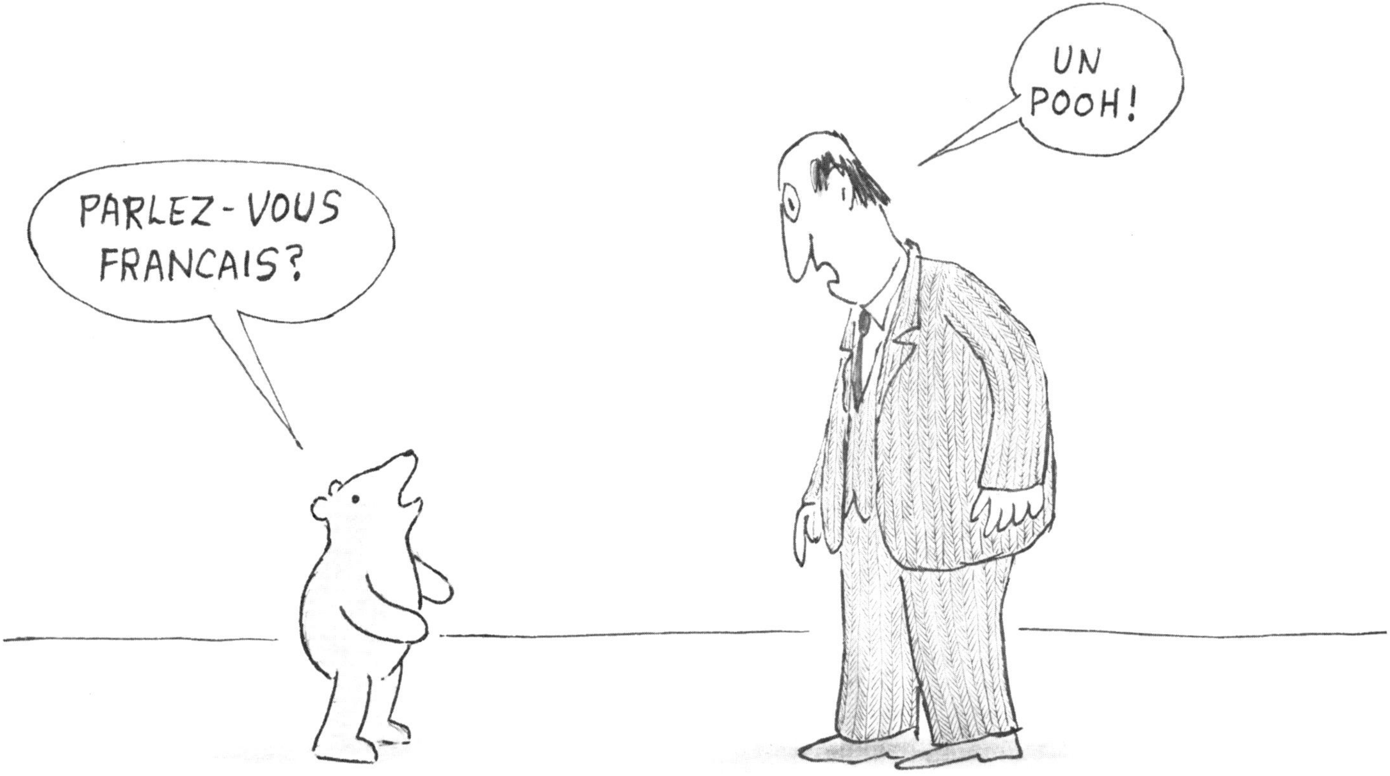
PARLEZ-VOUS FRANCAIS?
UN POOH!

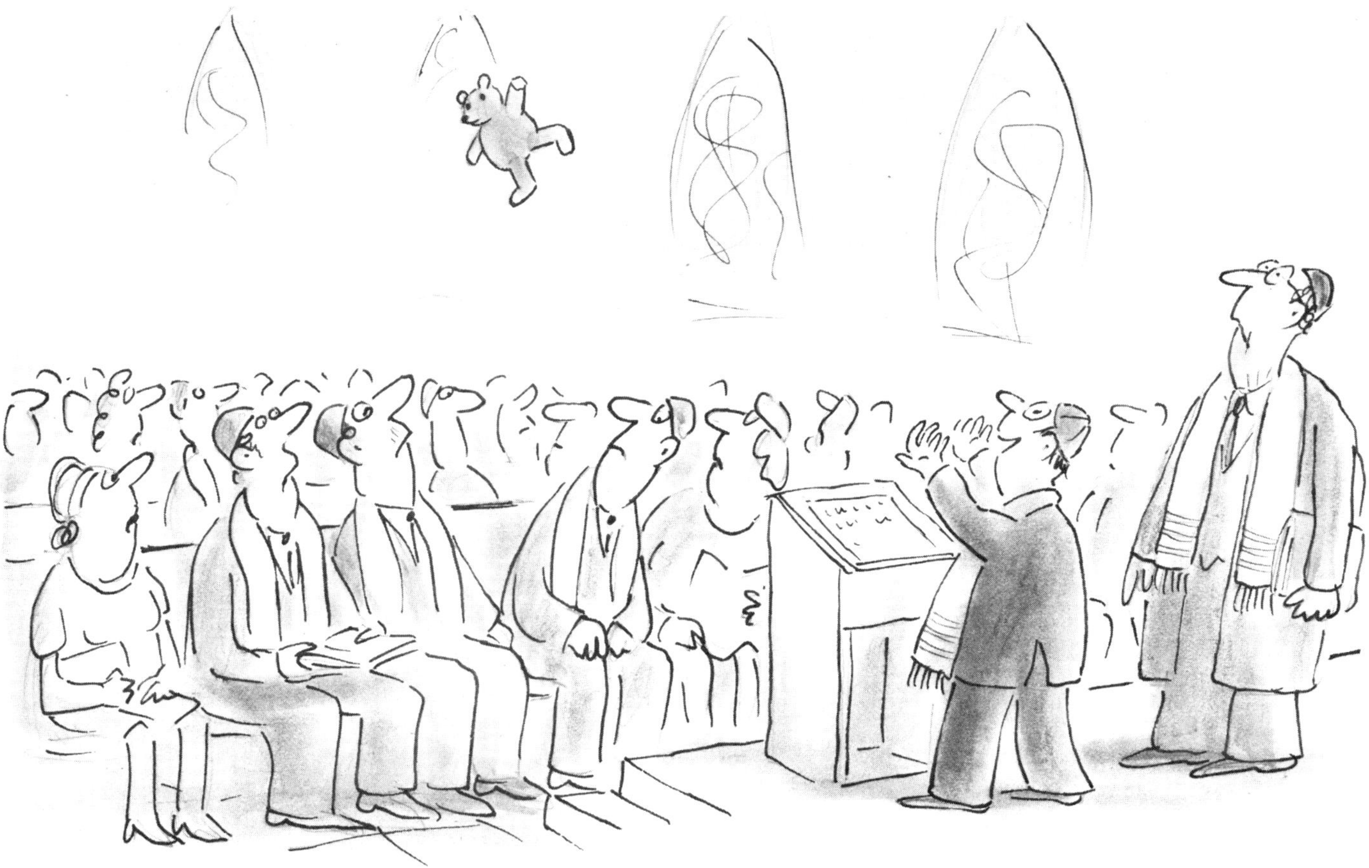

"Today I am a man."

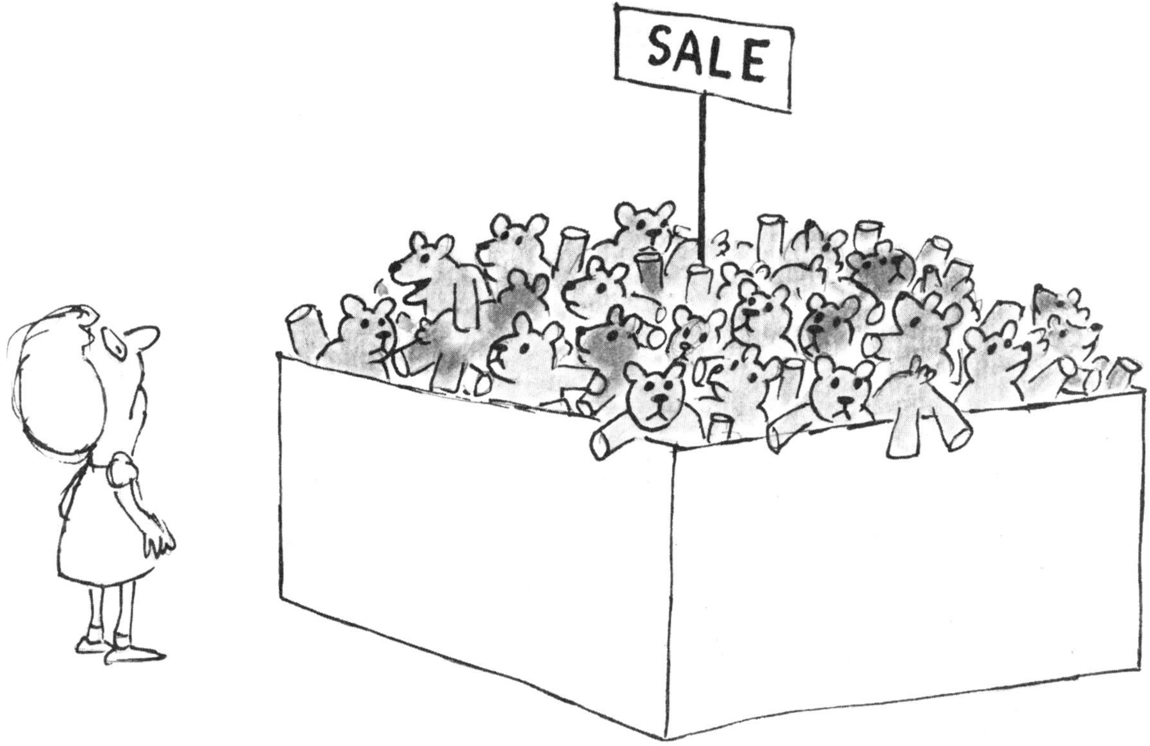
SALE

"Could you give us a few more minutes? We're having group sex."

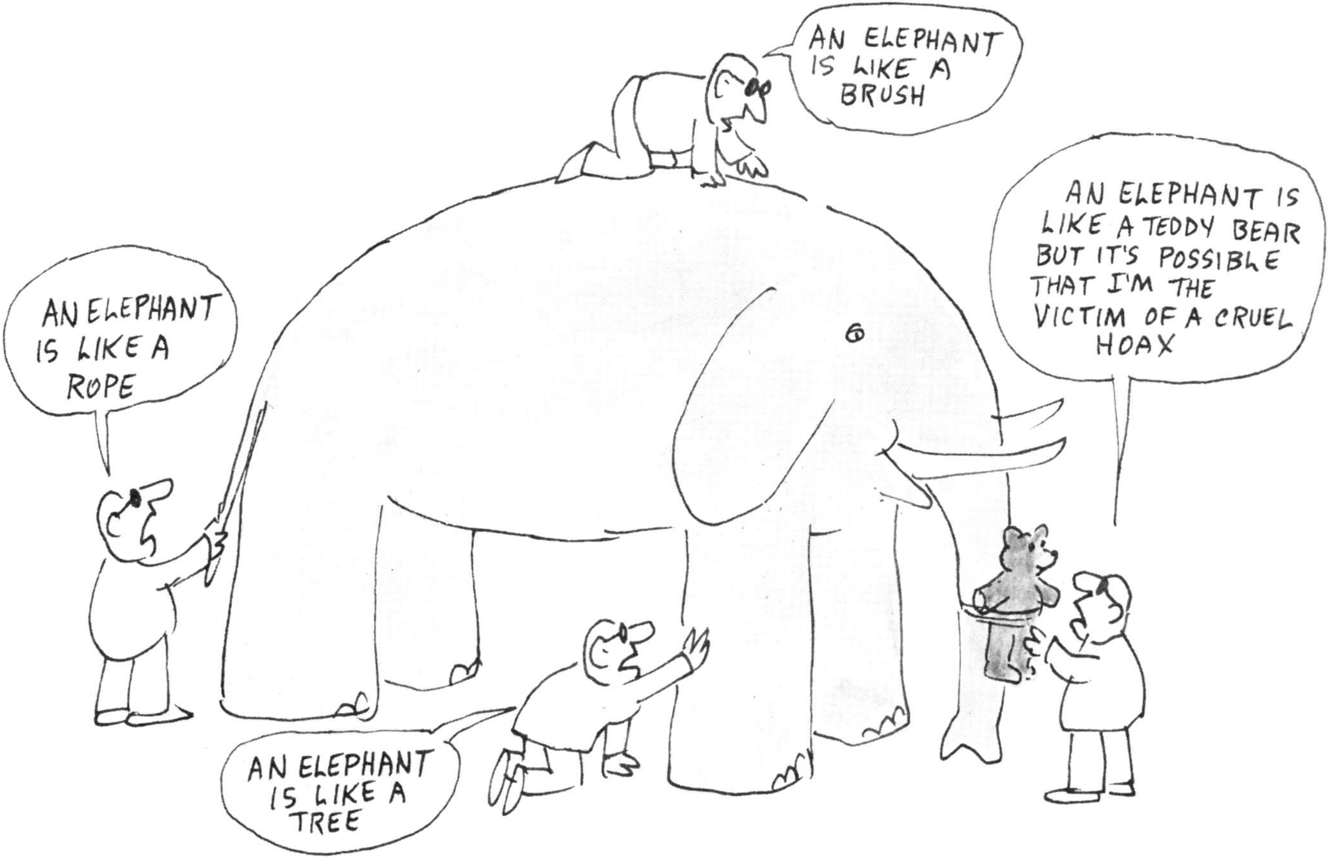
AN ELEPHANT IS LIKE A ROPE
AN ELEPHANT IS LIKE A BRUSH
AN ELEPHANT IS LIKE A TREE
AN ELEPHANT IS LIKE A TEDDY BEAR BUT IT'S POSSIBLE THAT I'M THE VICTIM OF A CRUEL HOAX

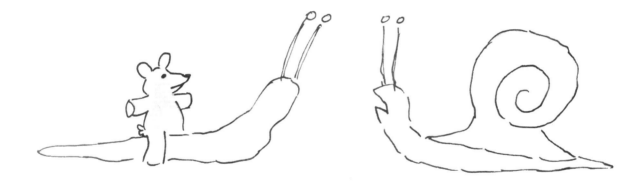

"Frankly, I prefer the security of a shell."

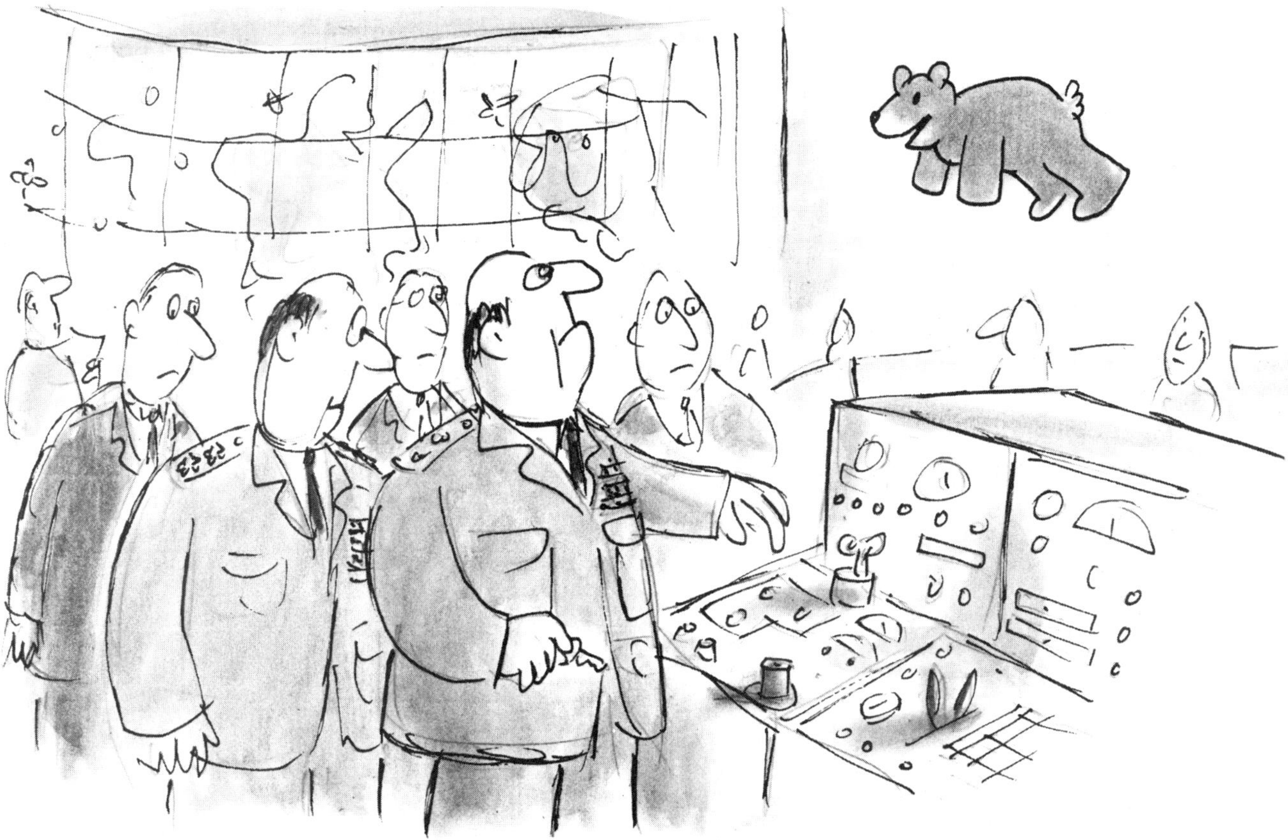

"Wait! Before you carry out your decision, spend a few minutes with me, your existential teddy bear."

"The little girl who owns you shall die, and you will be given to the Salvation Army."

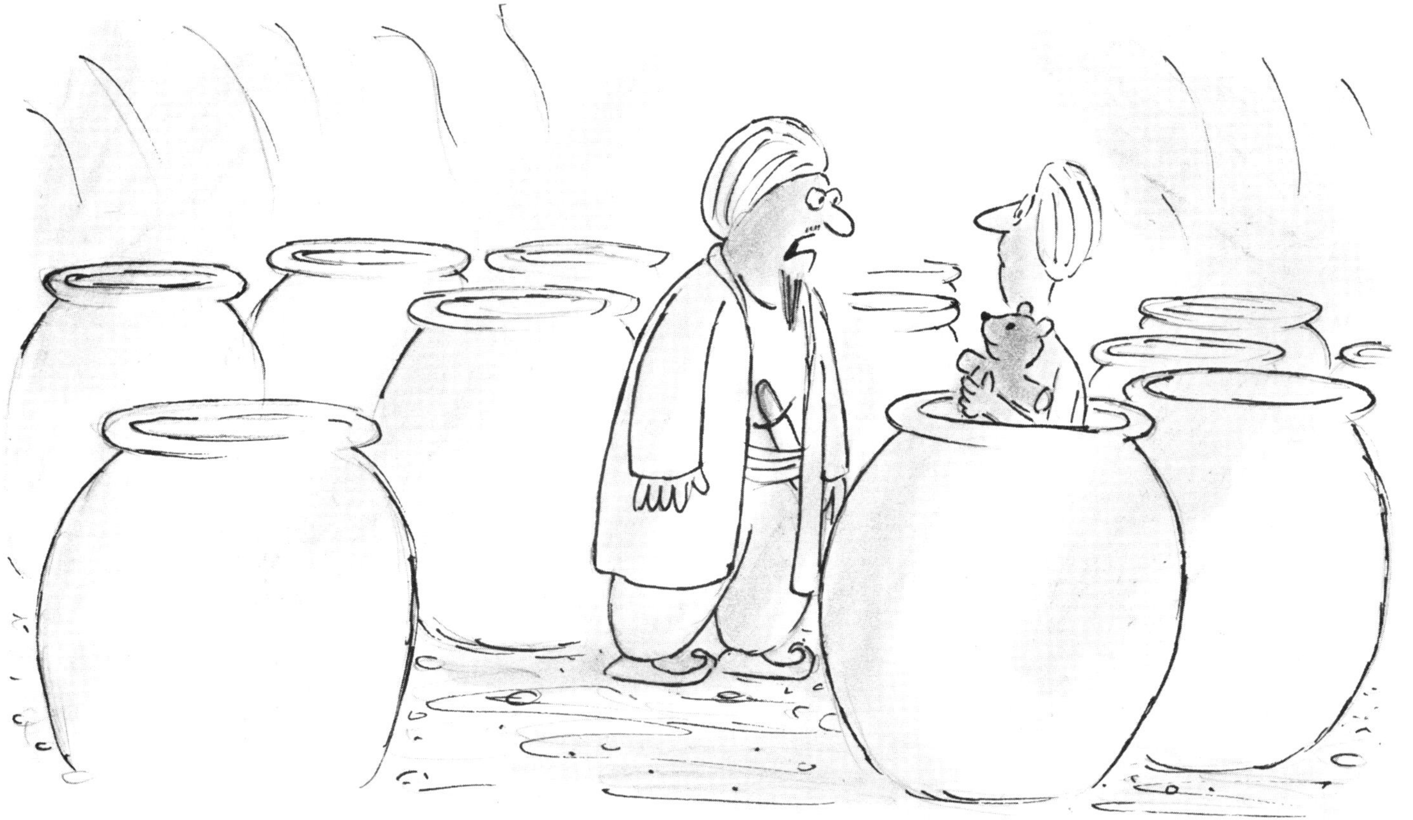

"Frankly, Achmed, I don't think you have the temperament to be a thief."

PARK HILL'S DOLL HOSPITAL
THE ETHEL AND HARRY SCHWARTZMAN
TEDDY BEAR WING

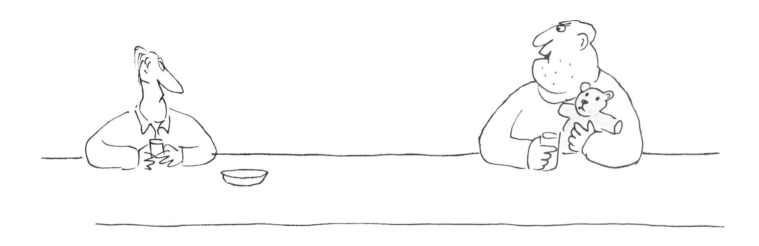

"It makes me look more sensitive and caring, which in turn helps me pick up girls."

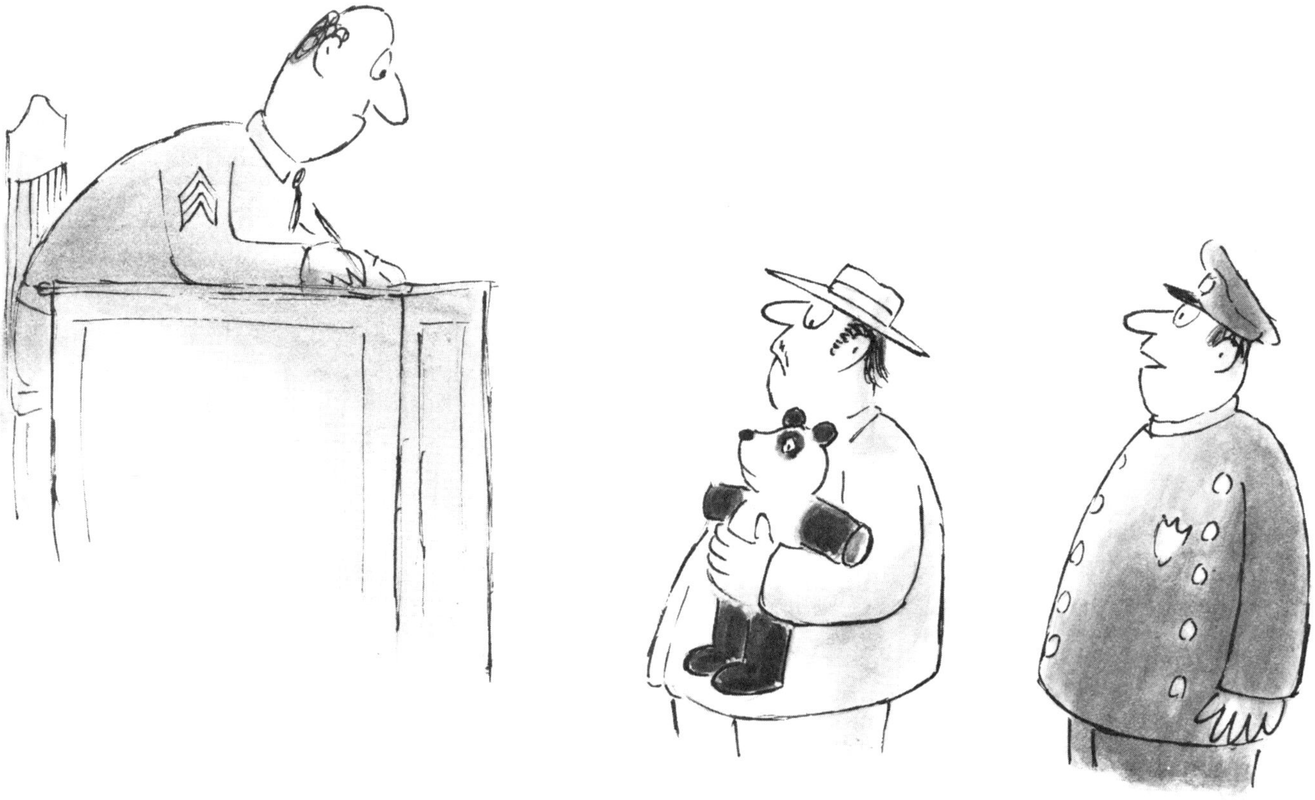

"I caught him pandering, Sarge."

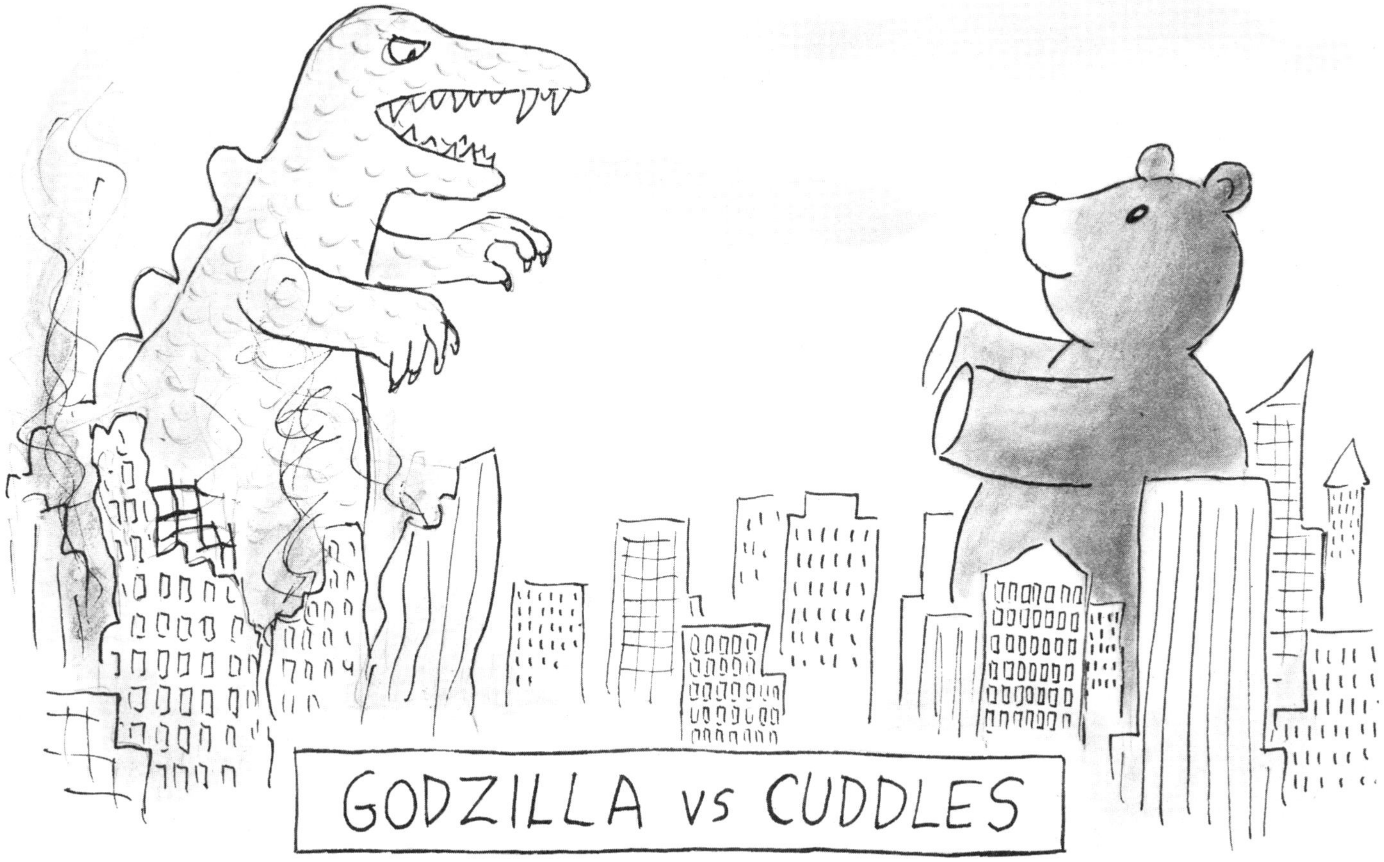
GODZILLA vs CUDDLES

"*Another nice thing about him is that he's always available when I need horsehair stuffing for my teddy bears.*"

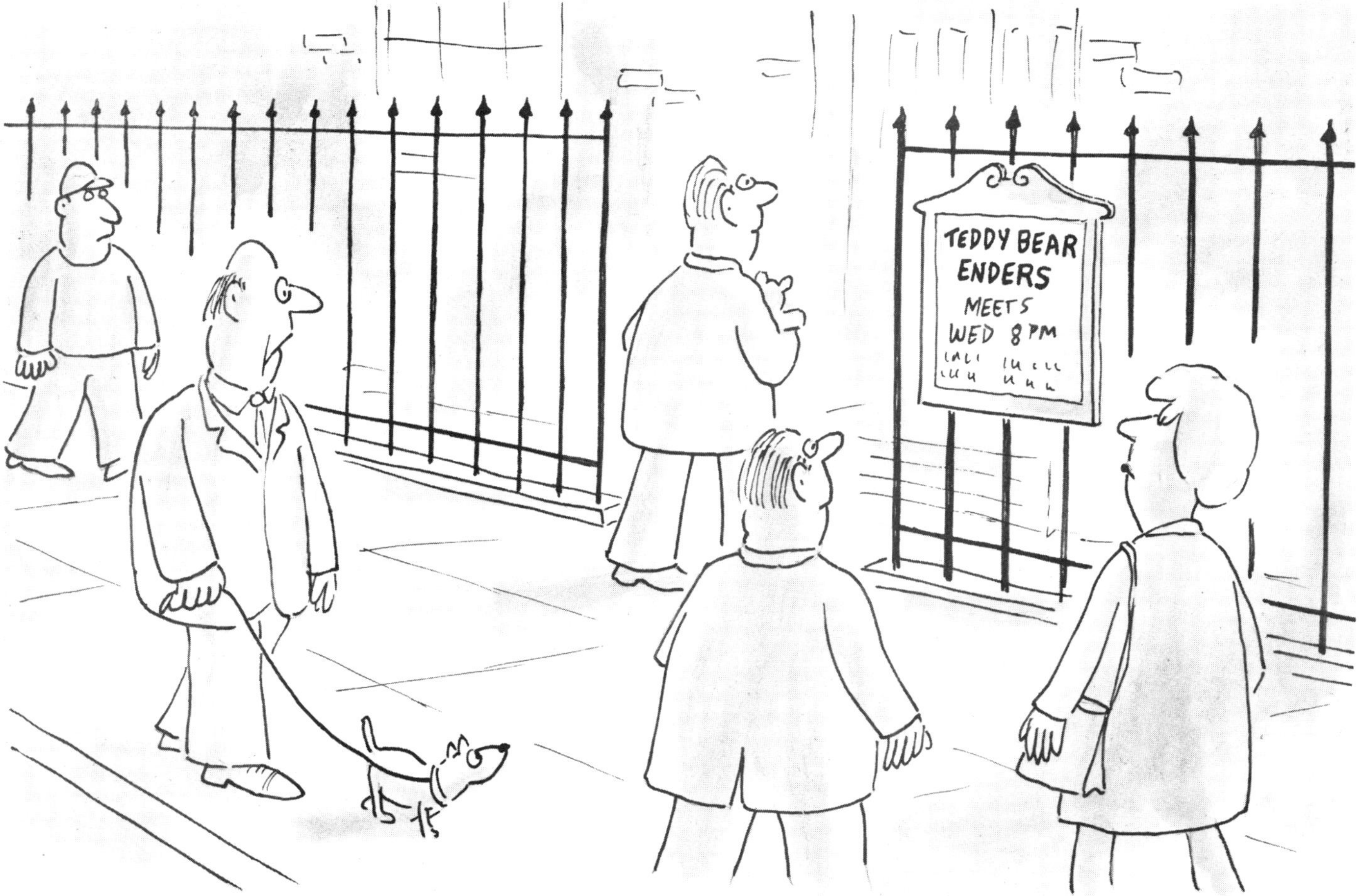
TEDDY BEAR
ENDERS
MEETS
WED 8 PM

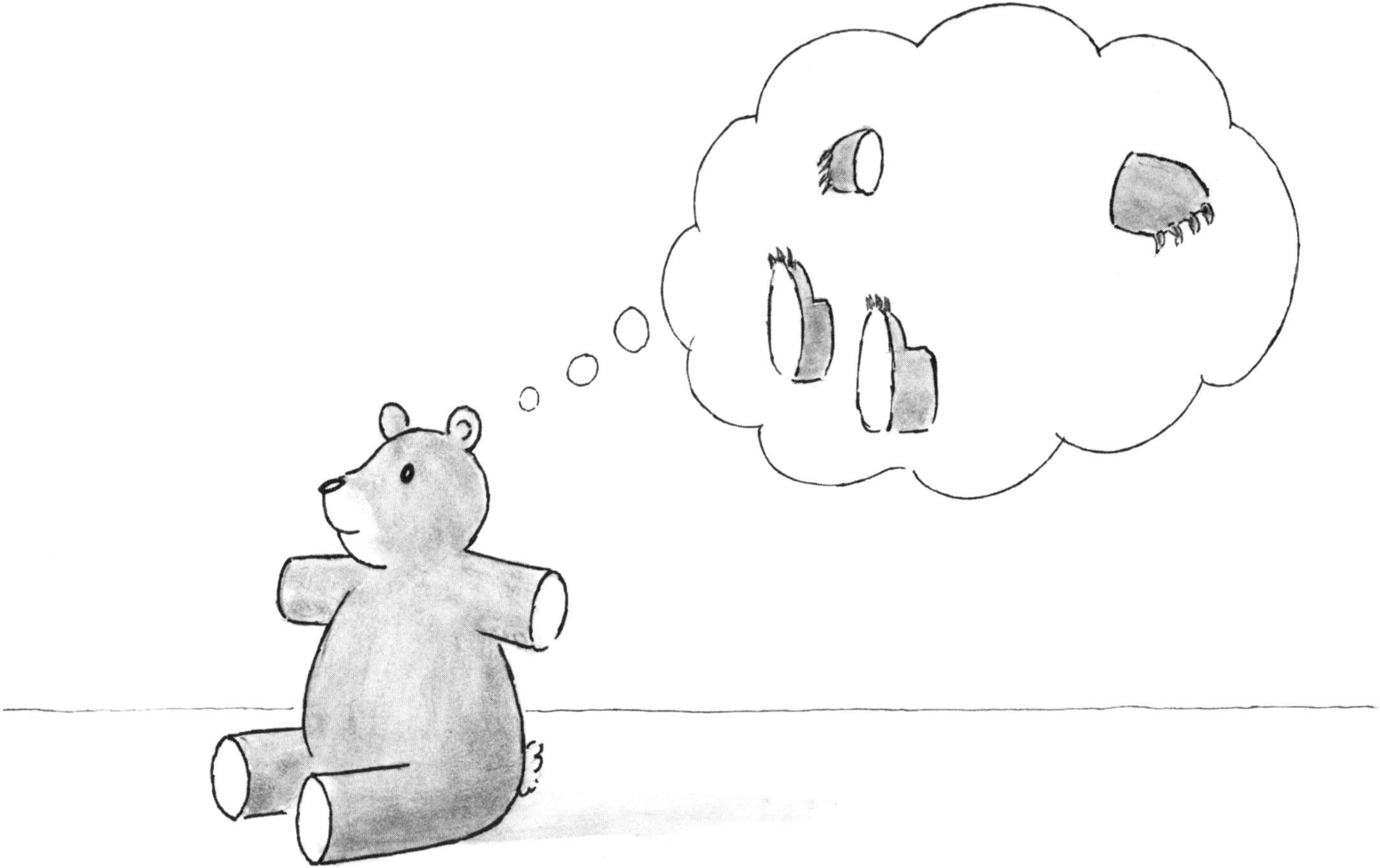

"On the contrary, I encourage the kids to bring them. Where I'm taking them, the rats use the stuffing to build nests."

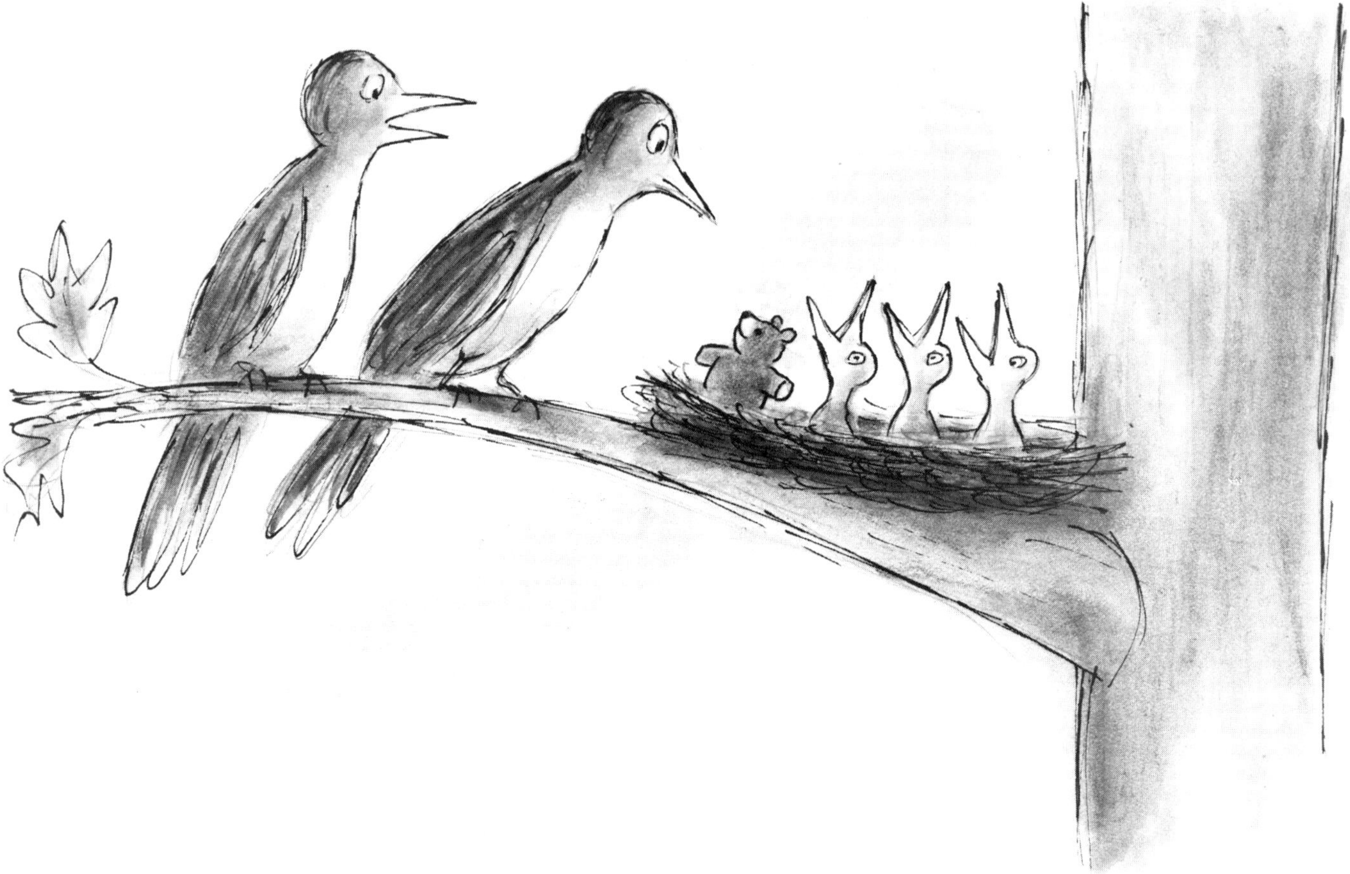

"Your mother brought it as a baby gift."

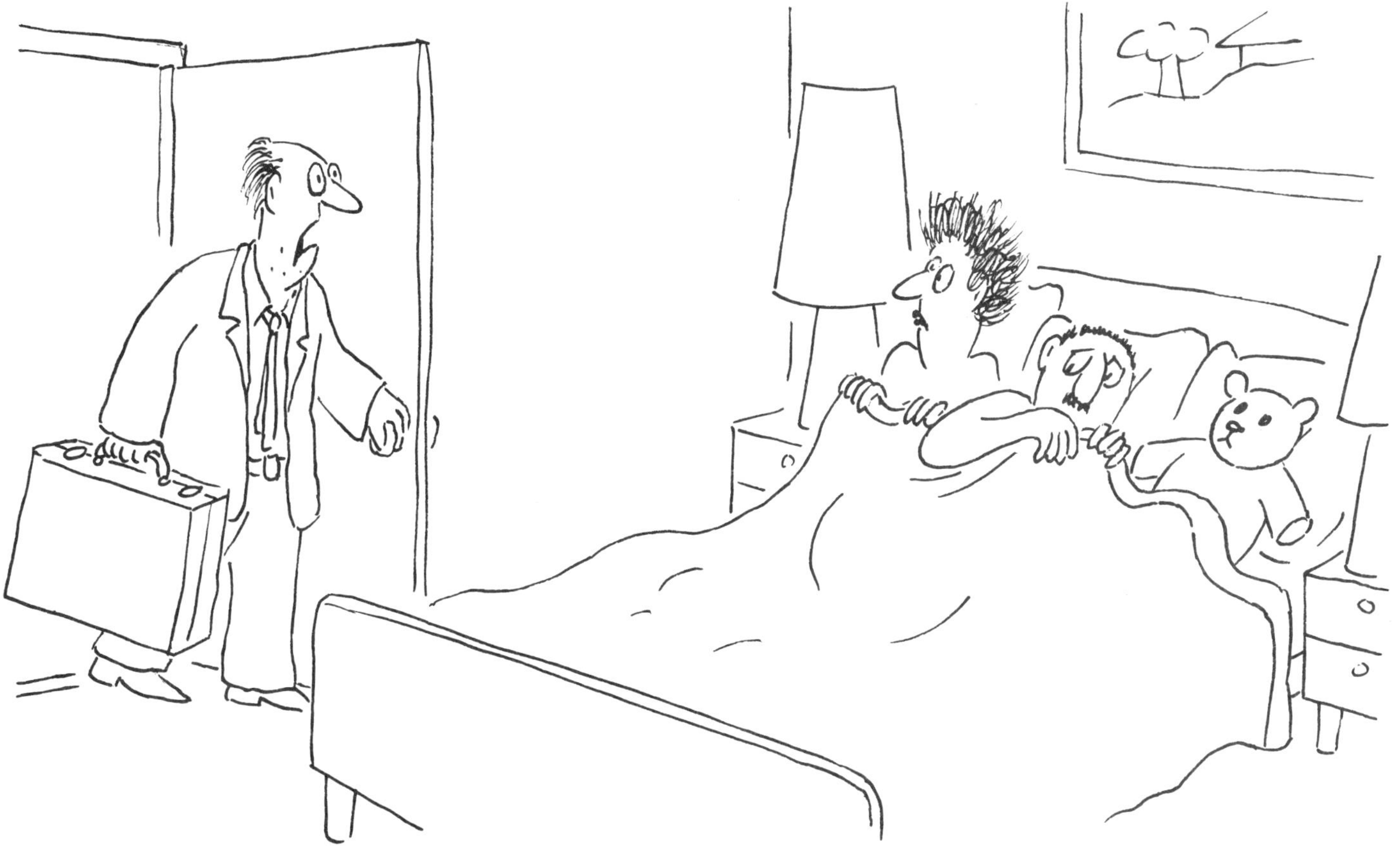

"My wife! My best friend! My teddy bear!"

"All I give is love and affection. If you want anything else you have to use a different lamp."

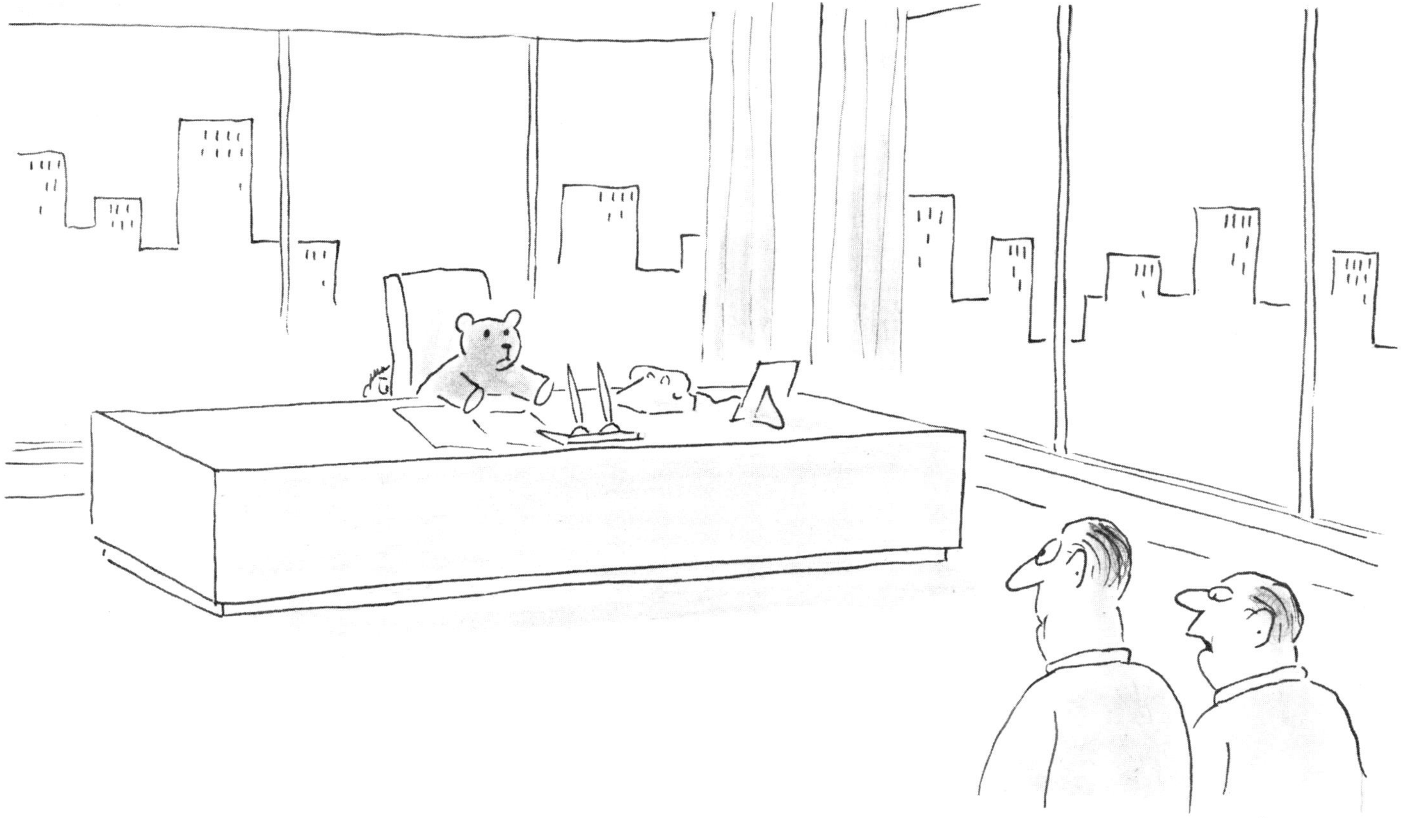

"Just humor him until the next board meeting."

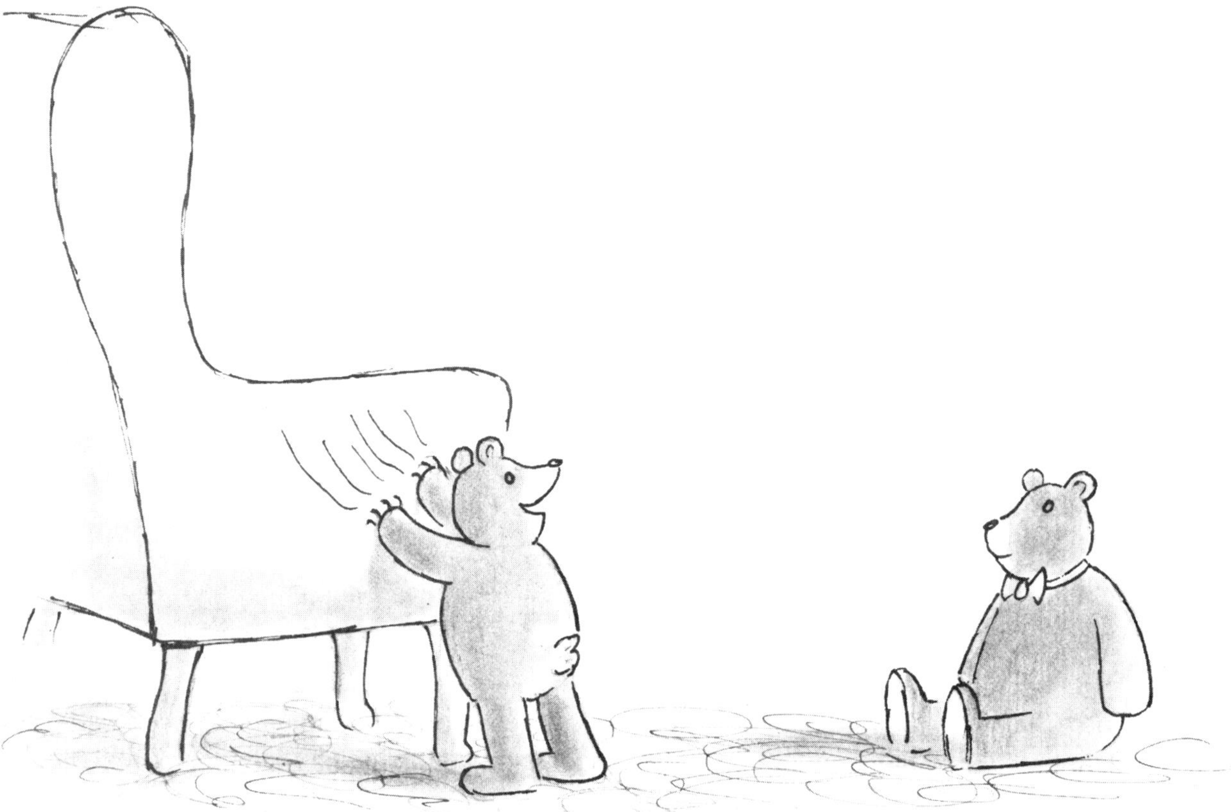

"They'll blame it on the cat."

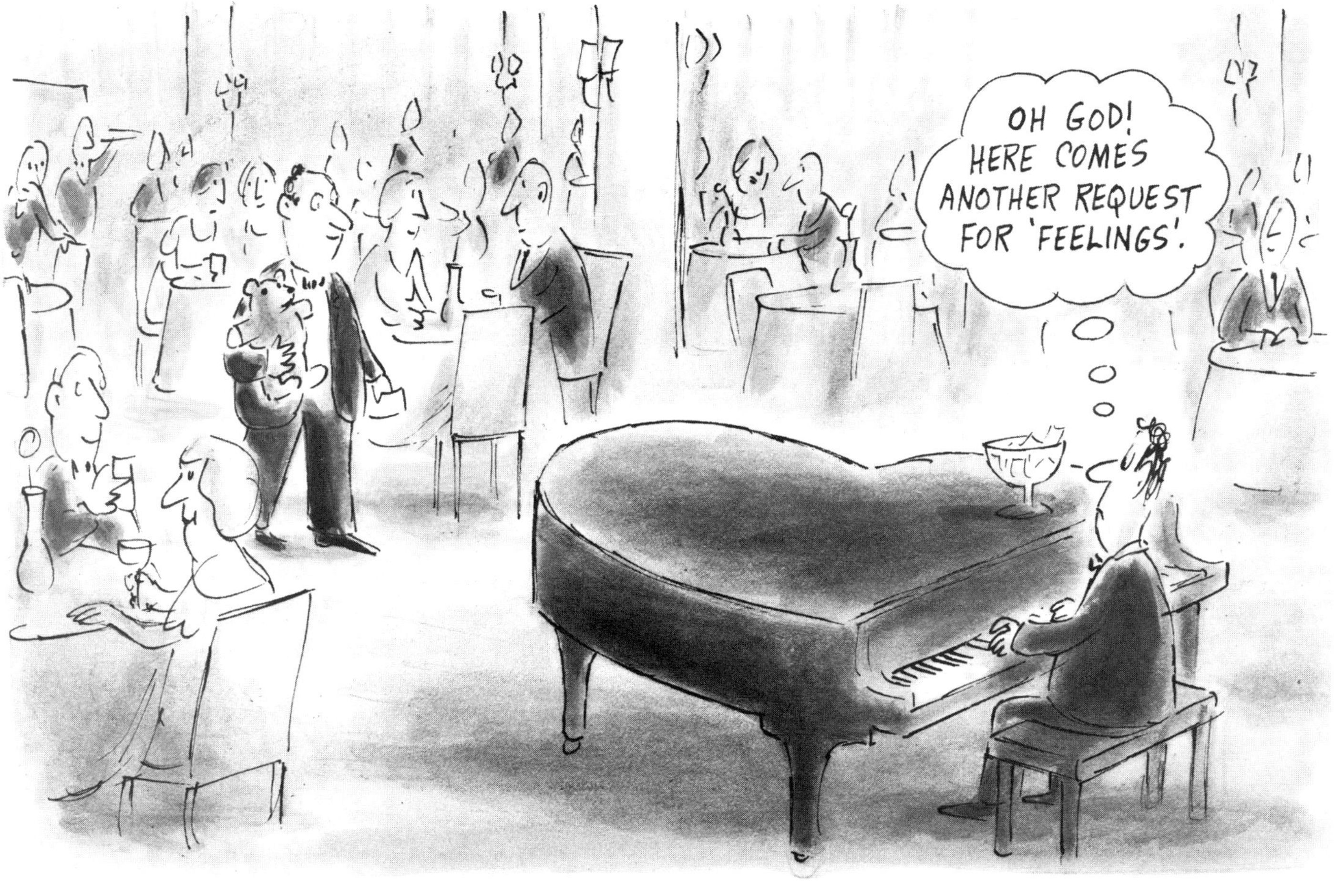
OH GOD! HERE COMES ANOTHER REQUEST FOR 'FEELINGS'.

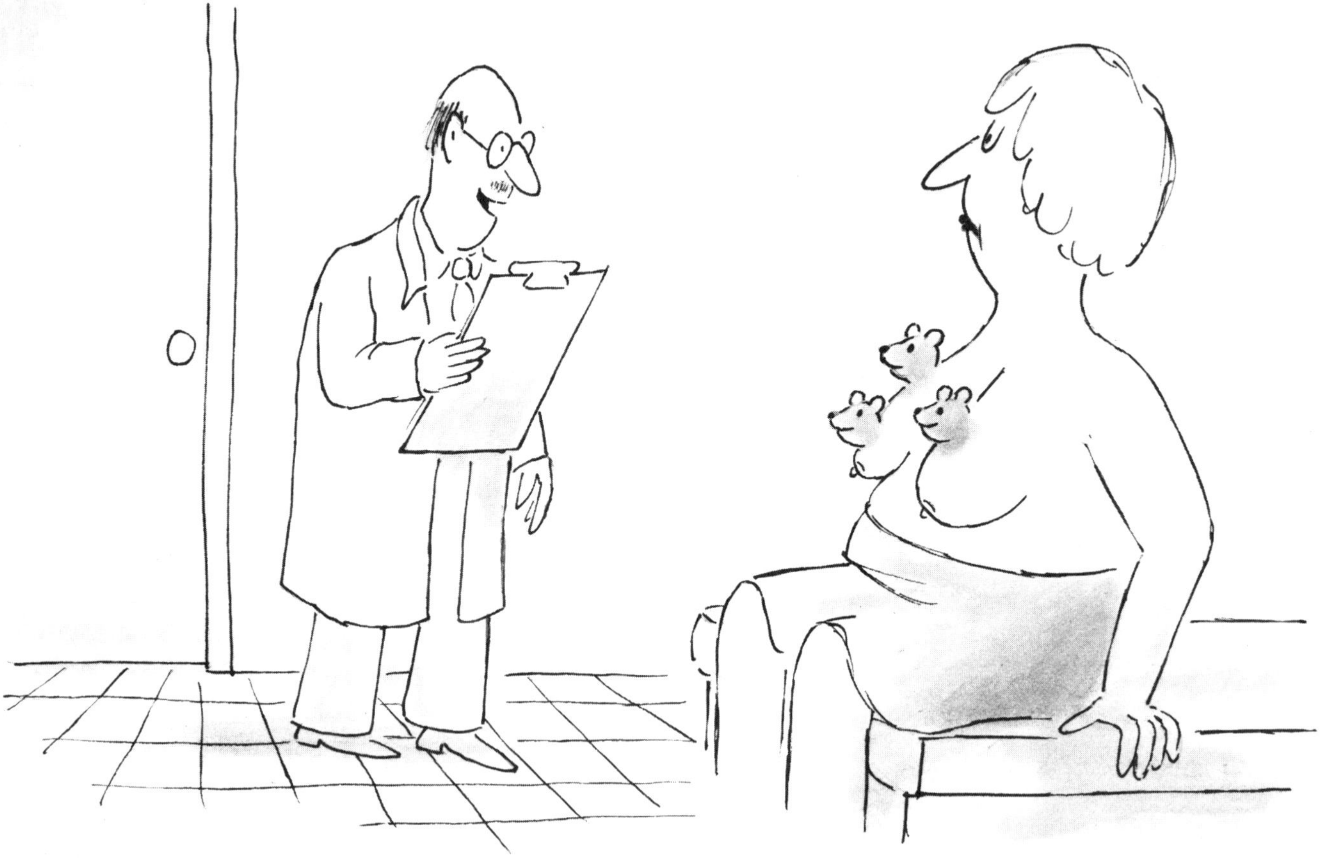

"Good news, Mrs. Mostyn. The tests show that they're benign."

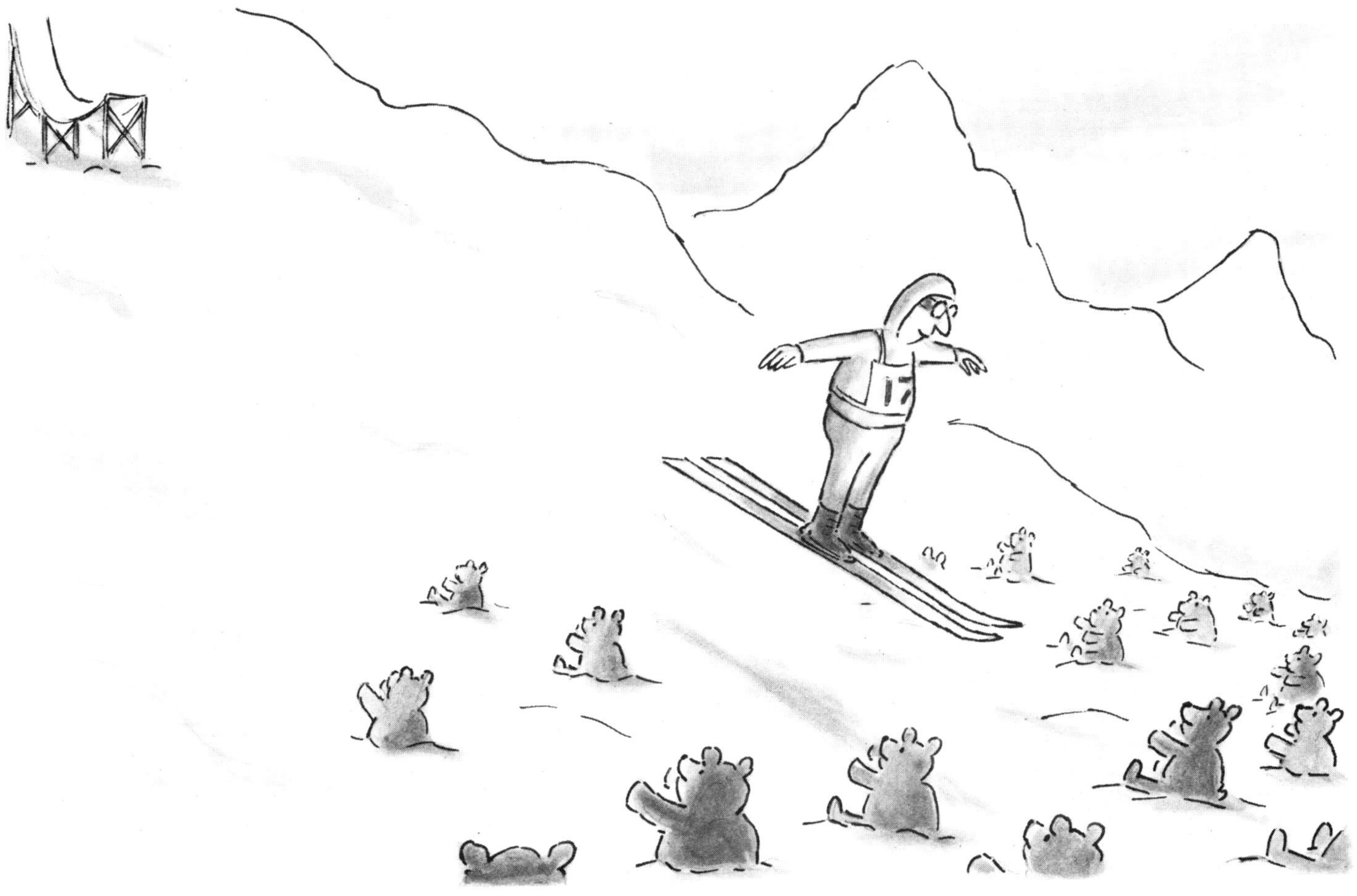

17

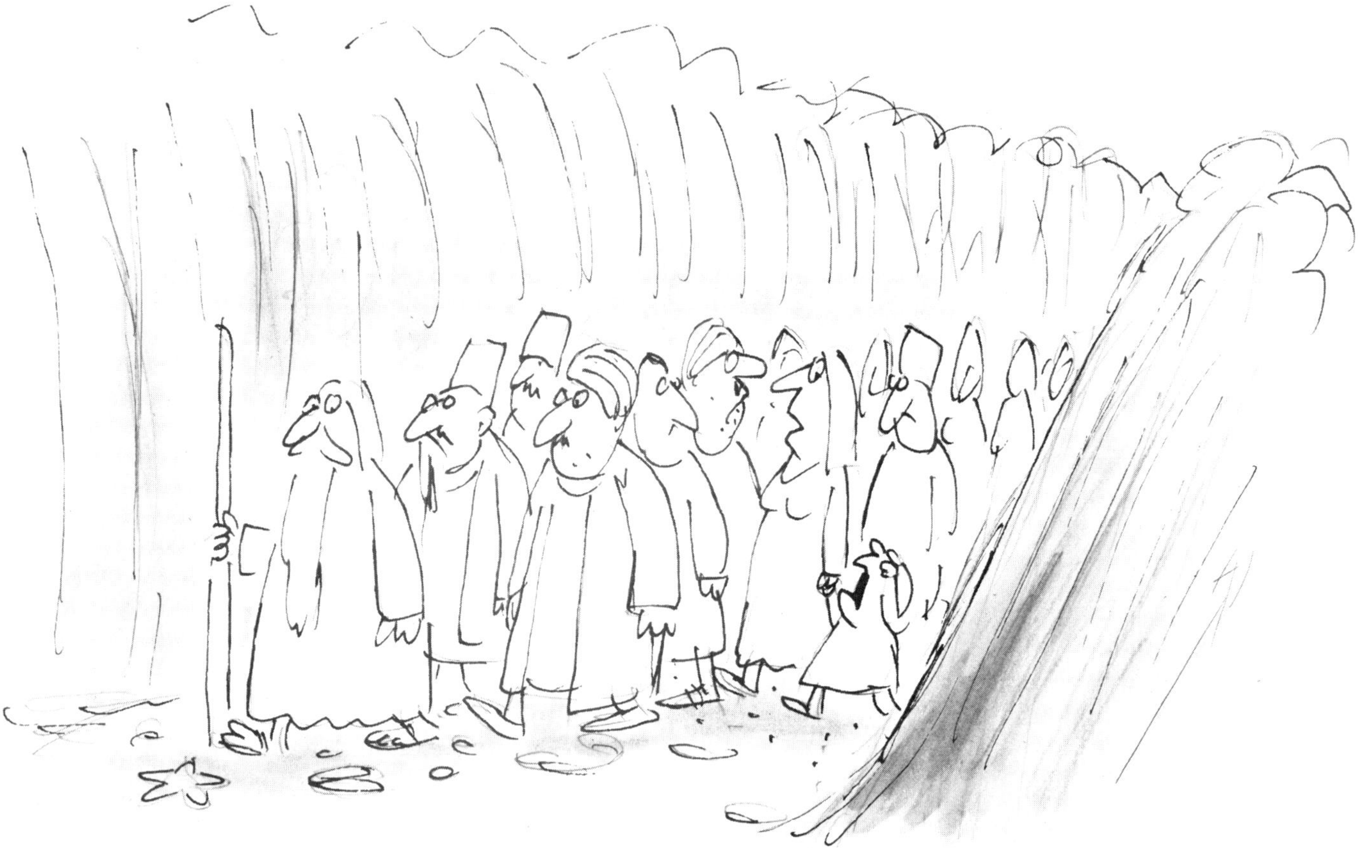

"We have to go back. He left his teddy bear."

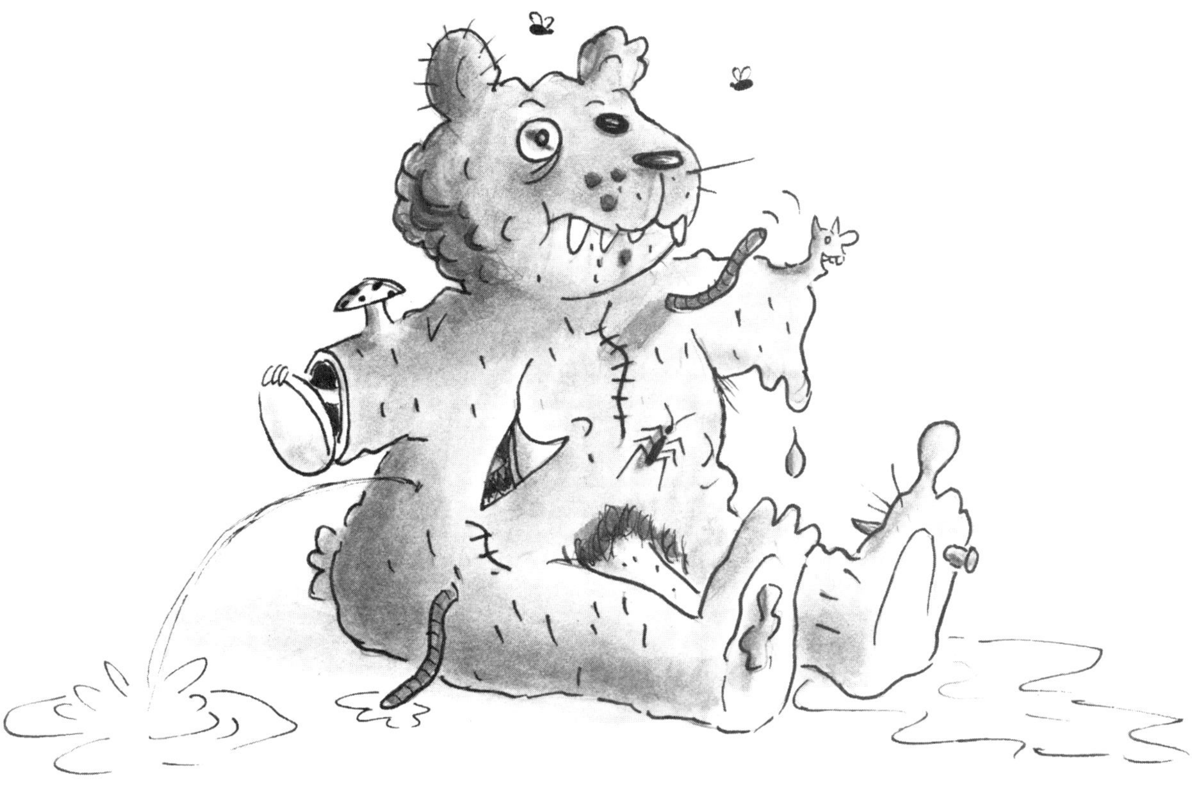

The Teddy Bear of Dorian Gray

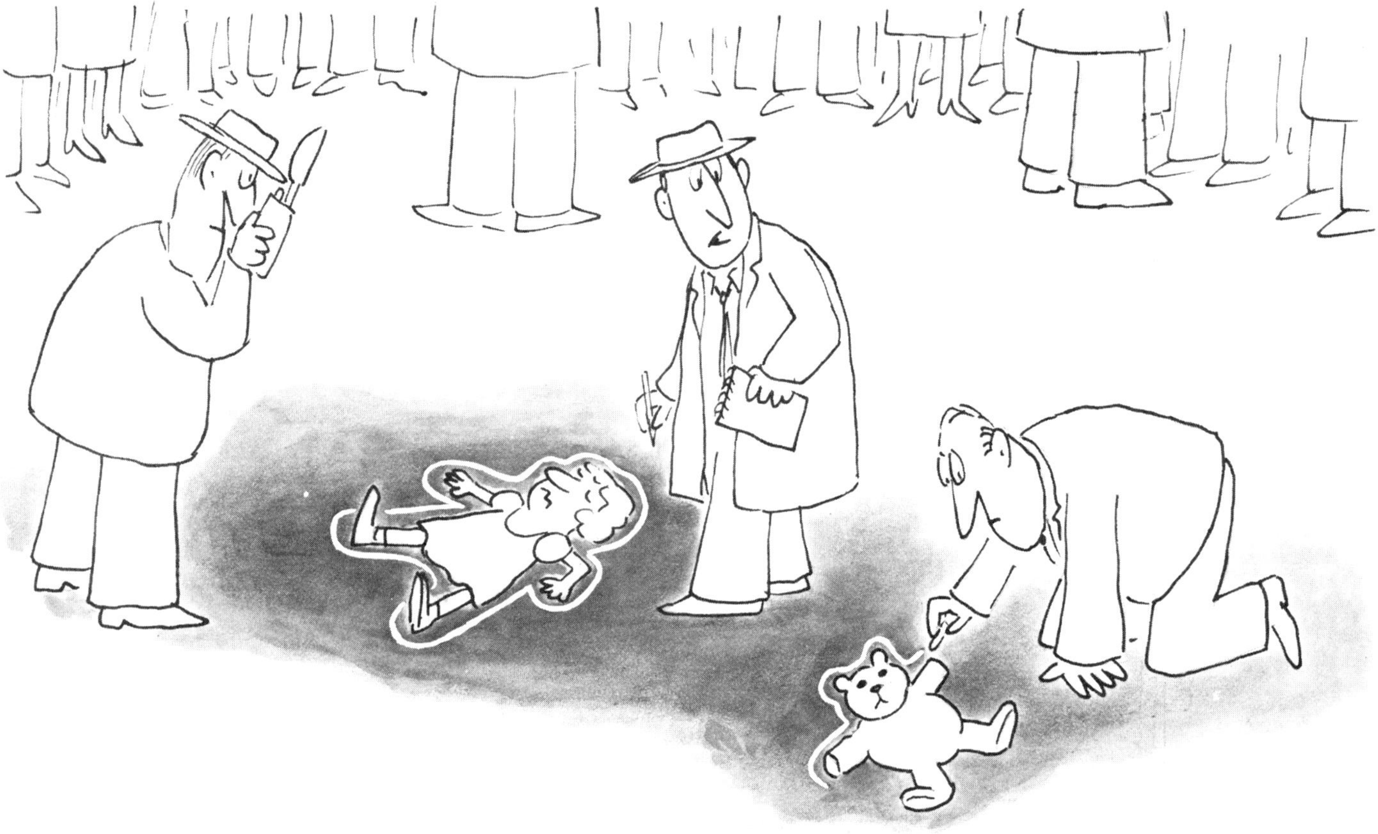

"That won't be necessary, Dooley."

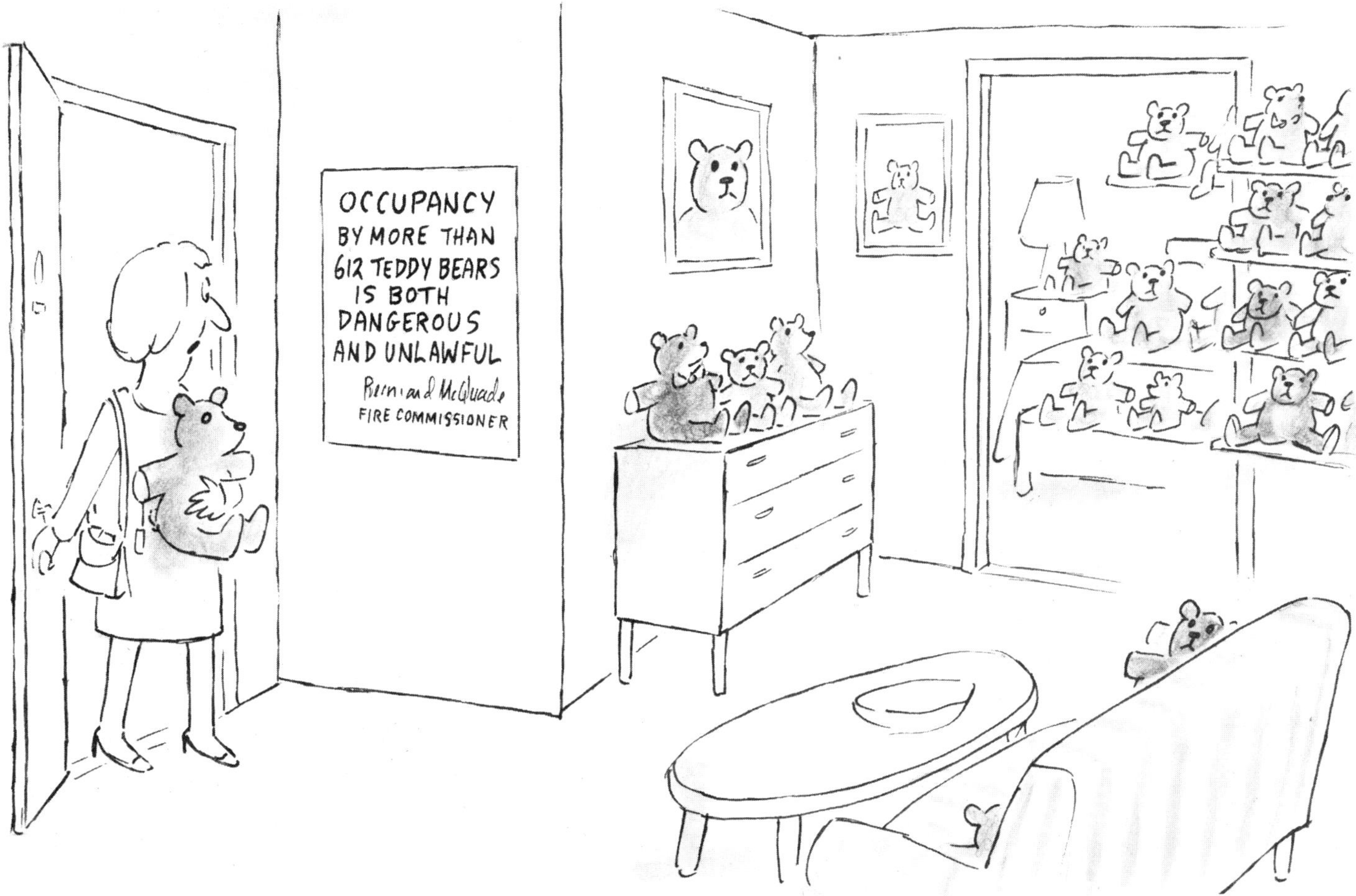
OCCUPANCY
BY MORE THAN
612 TEDDY BEARS
IS BOTH
DANGEROUS
AND UNLAWFUL
Bernard McQuade
FIRE COMMISSIONER

"J'accuse!"

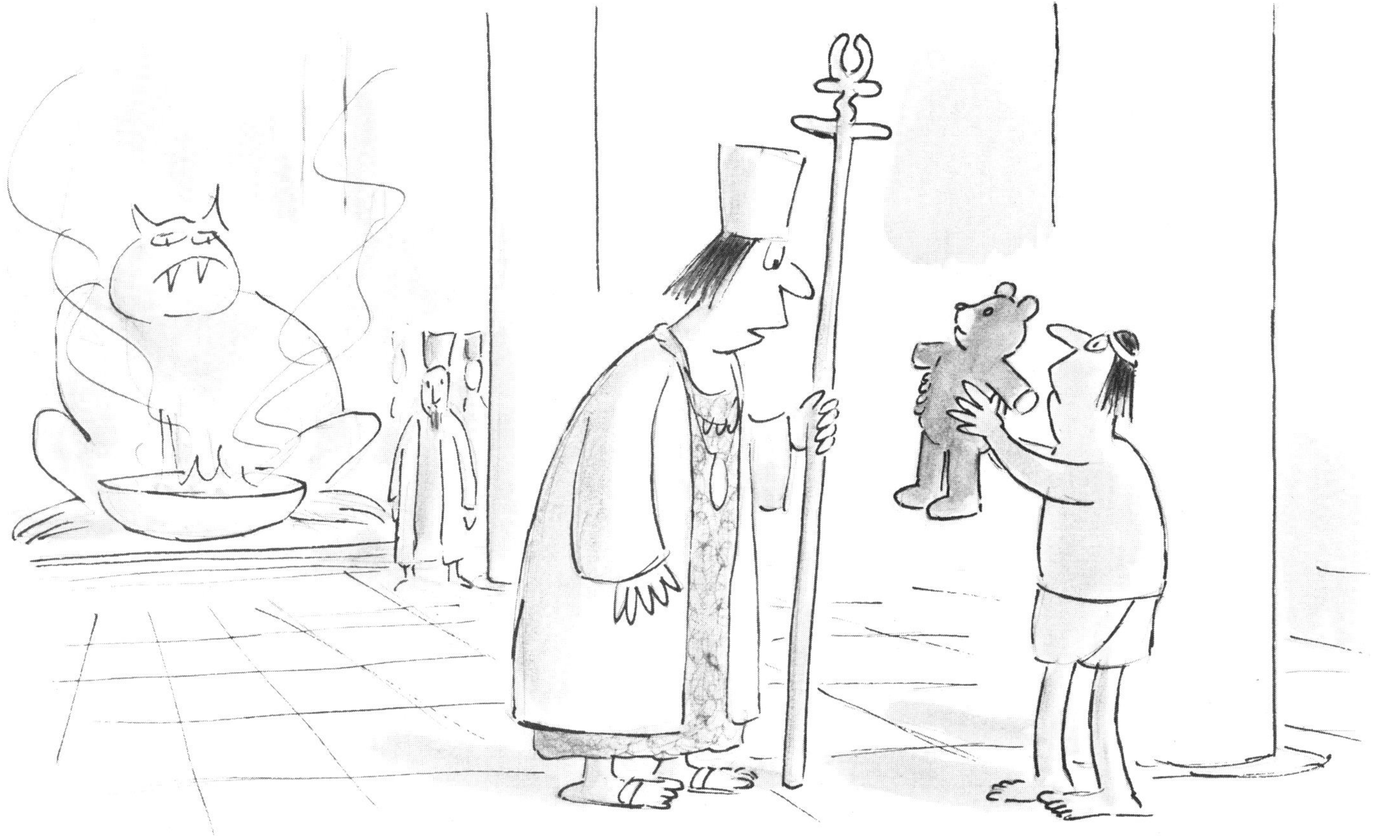

"We appreciate the gesture, but you're still going to have to offer up your first born as a sacrifice."

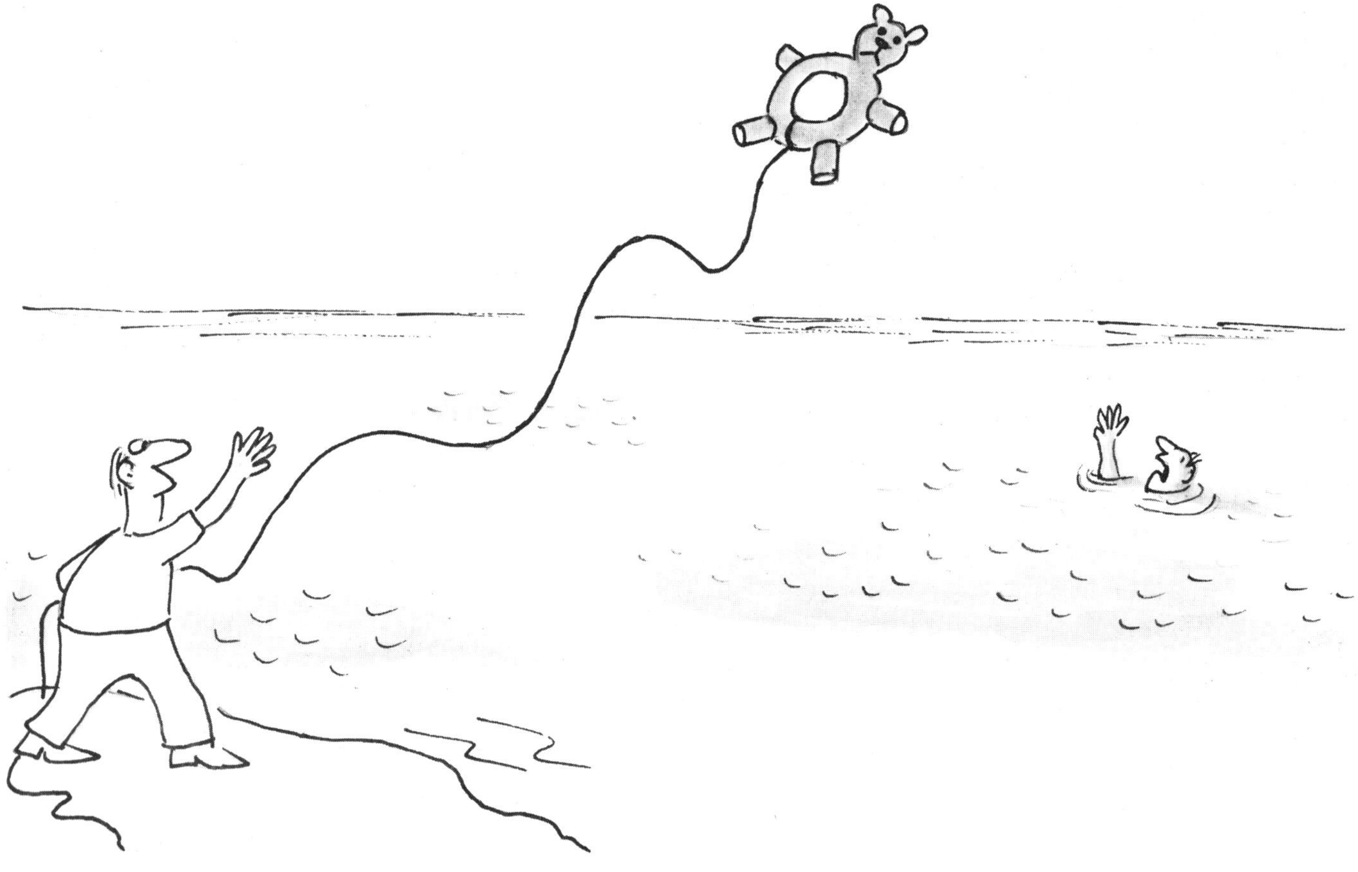

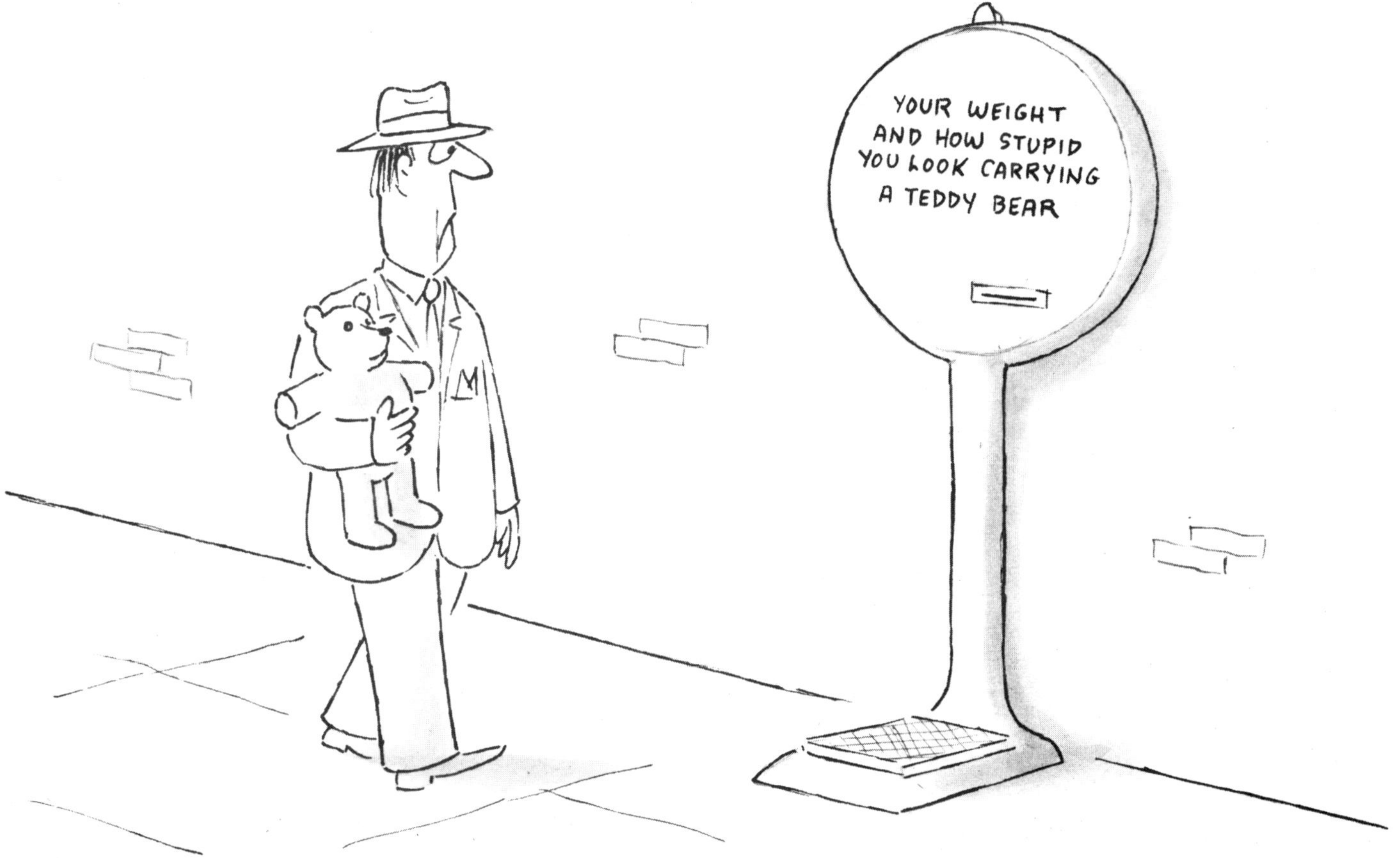
YOUR WEIGHT
AND HOW STUPID
YOU LOOK CARRYING
A TEDDY BEAR

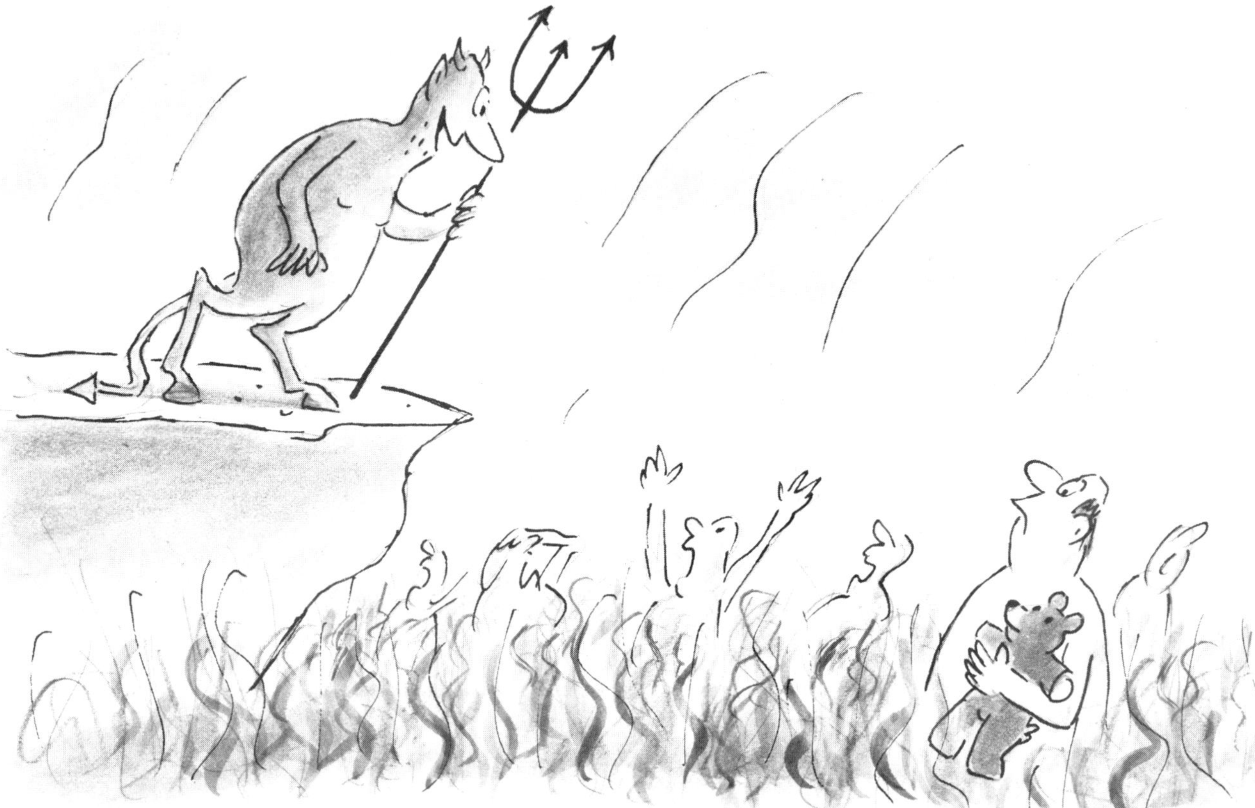

"Guess who's going to be asked to give up his teddy bear."

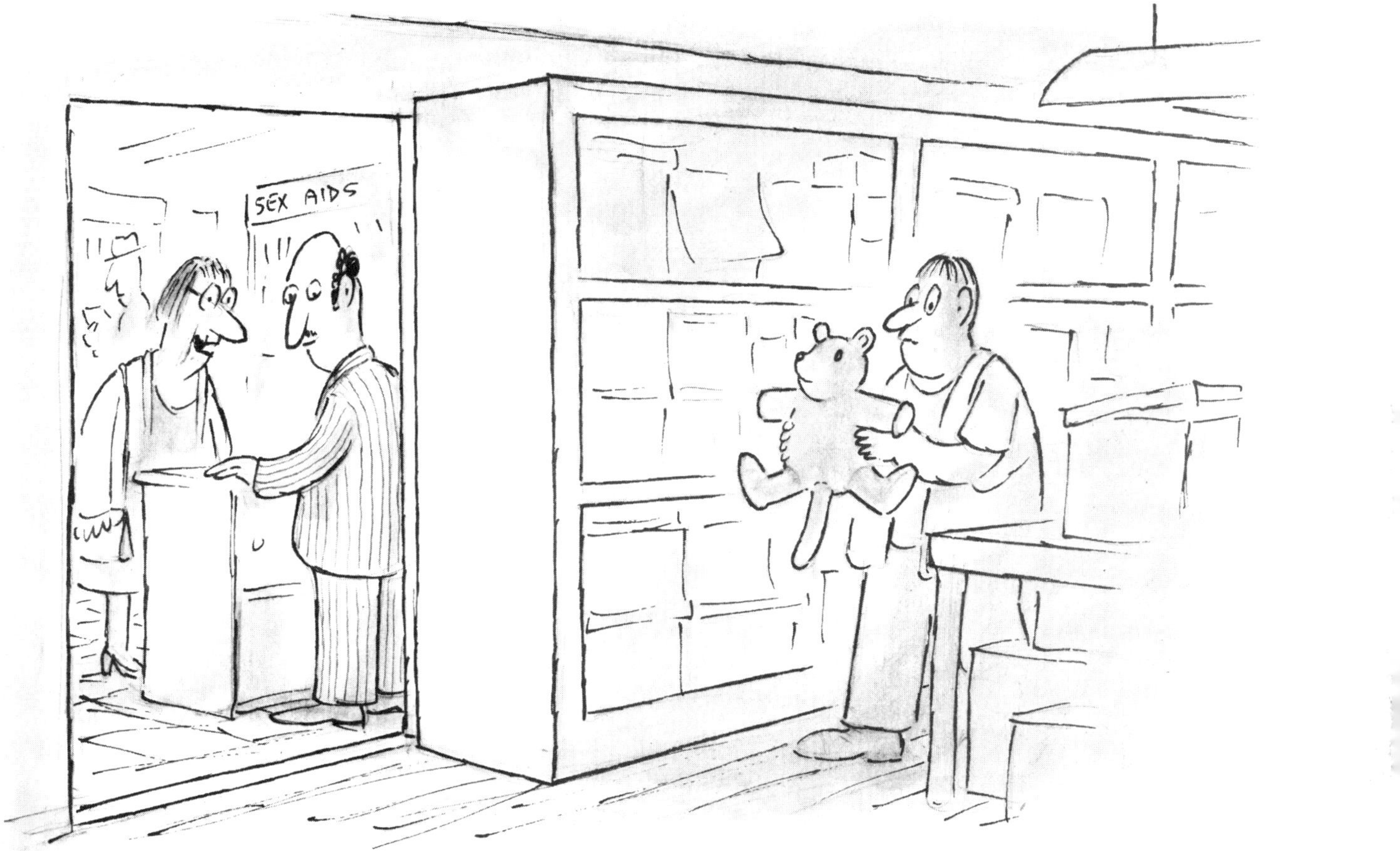
SEX AIDS

"$350 for a dildo? What's it made out of, gold?"

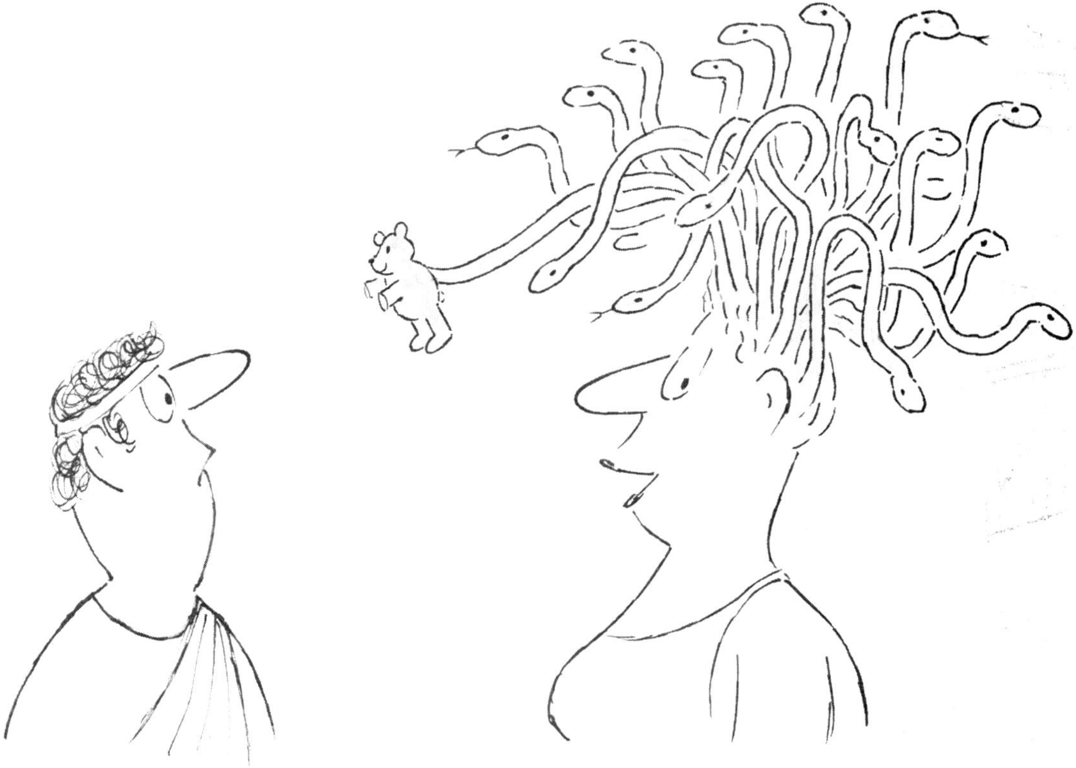

"I'm trying to improve my image."

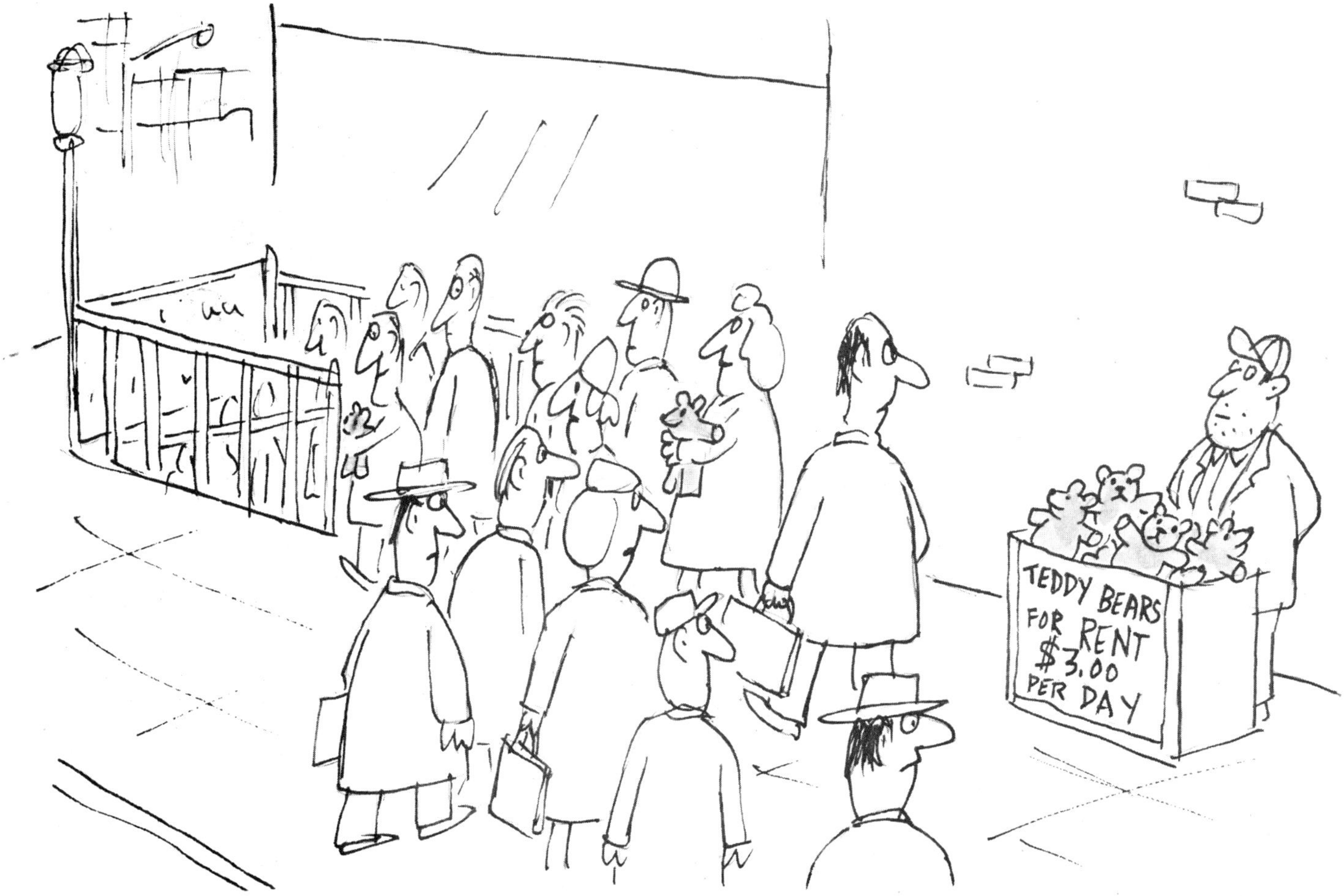
TEDDY BEARS
FOR RENT
$3.00
PER DAY

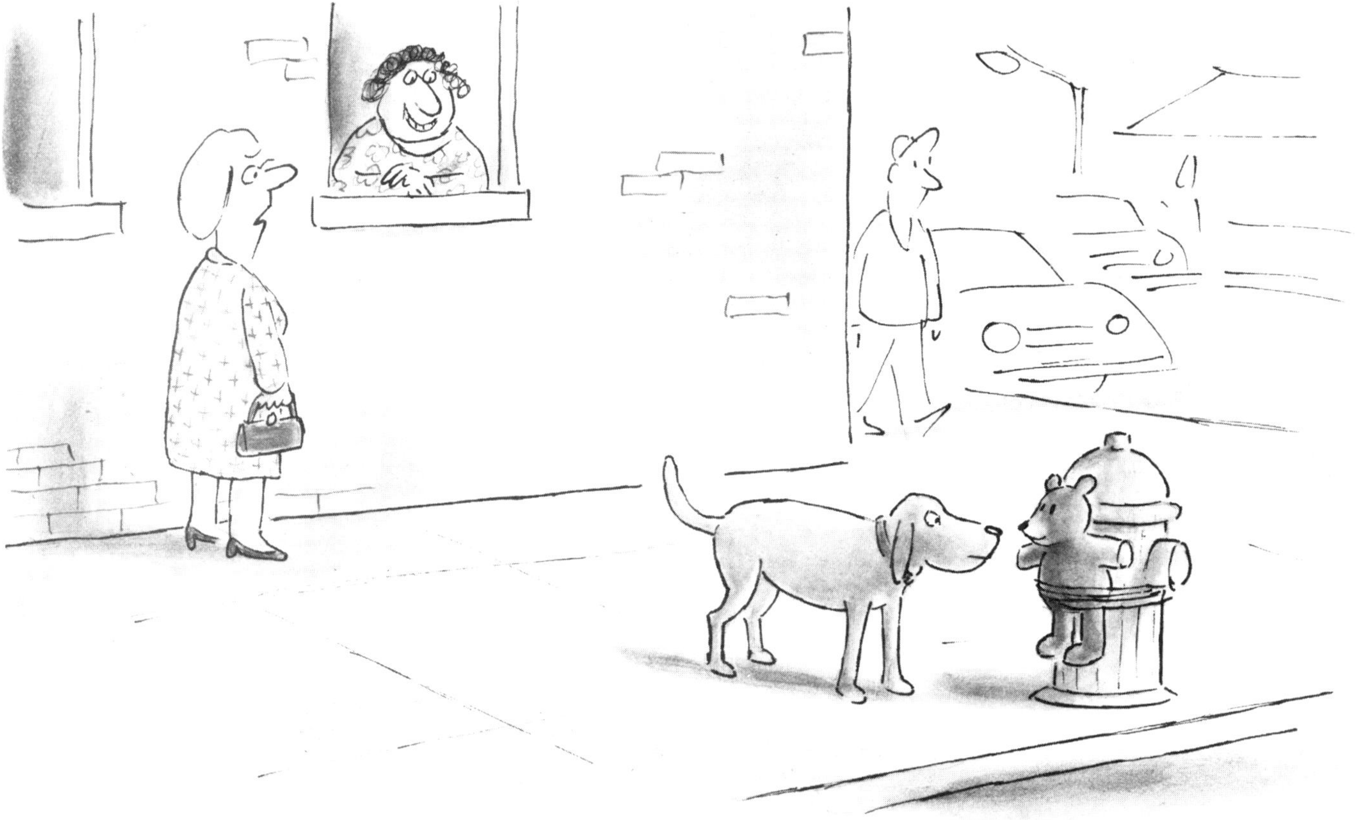

"Gosh! You must really hate the guy to do that to his teddy bear."

"*Just you, Pinocchio. My experience with teddy bears is that when they're changed into real bears, they become quite vicious.*"

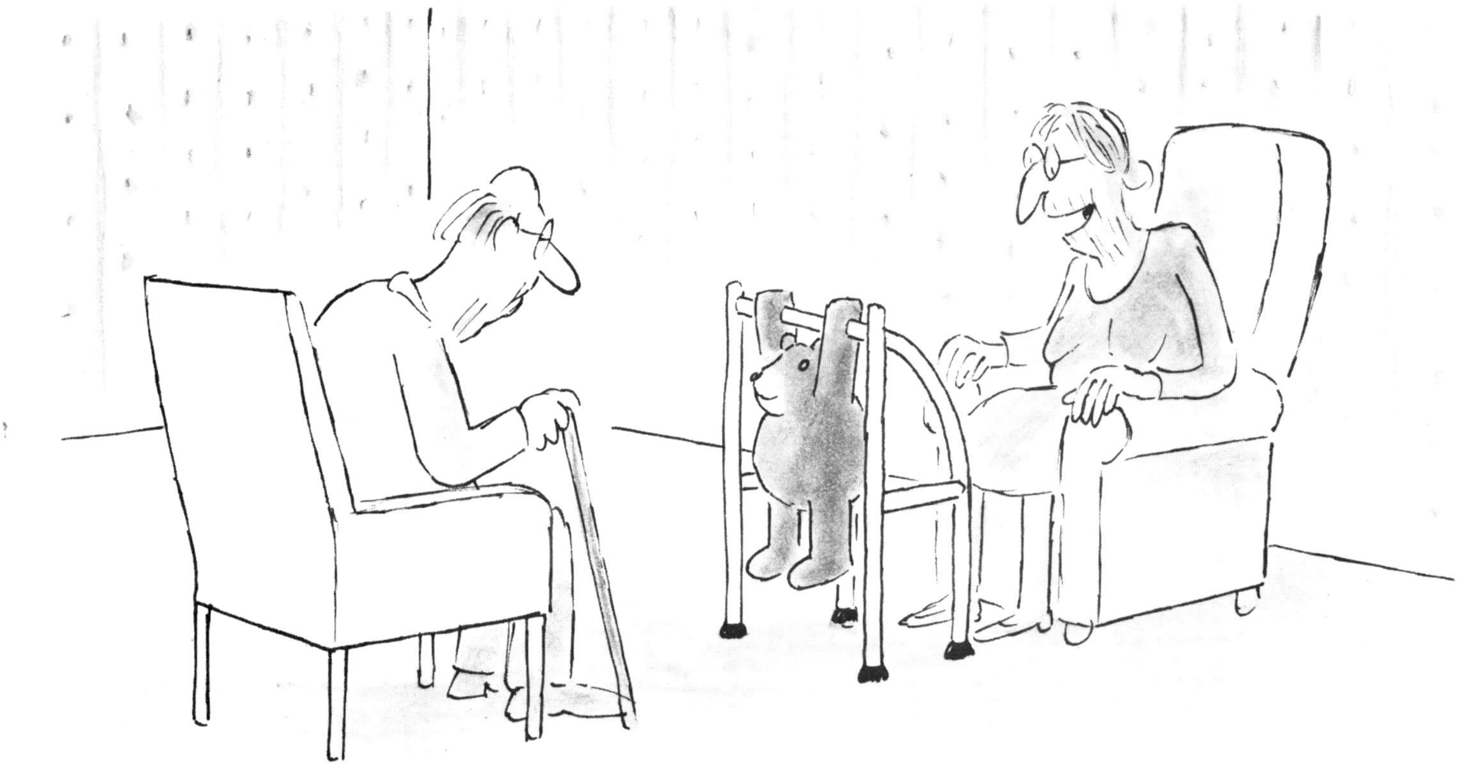

"'Bear' and I have grown old together."

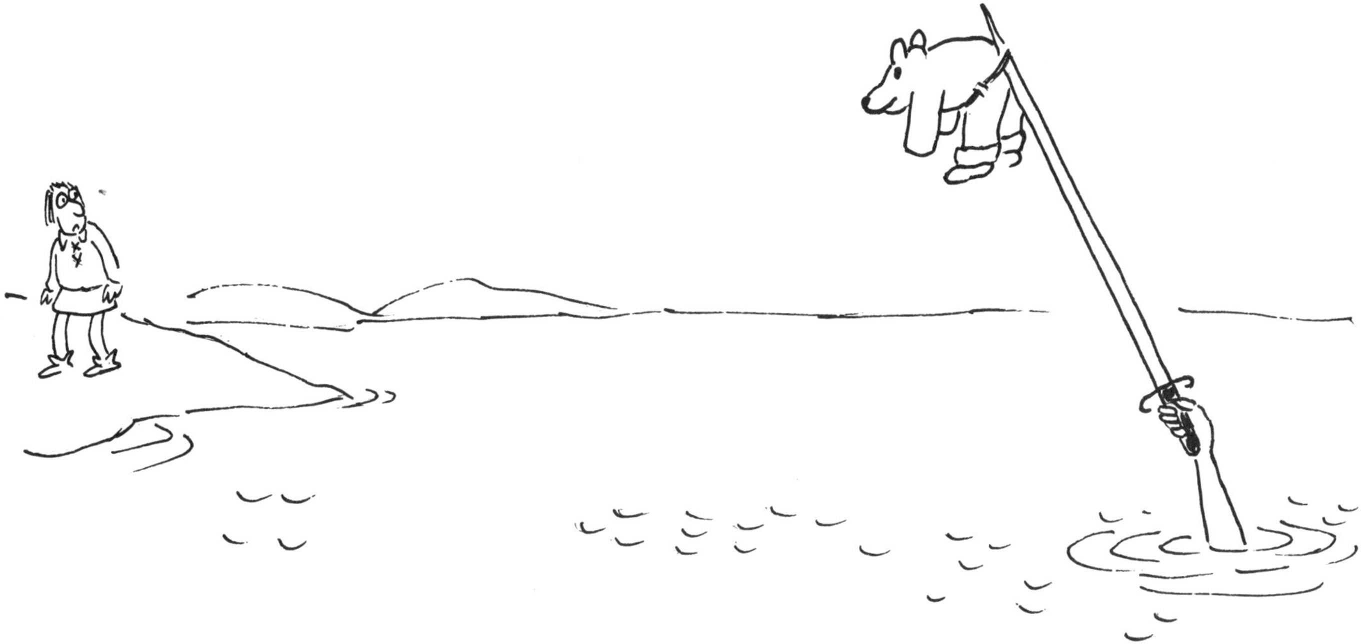

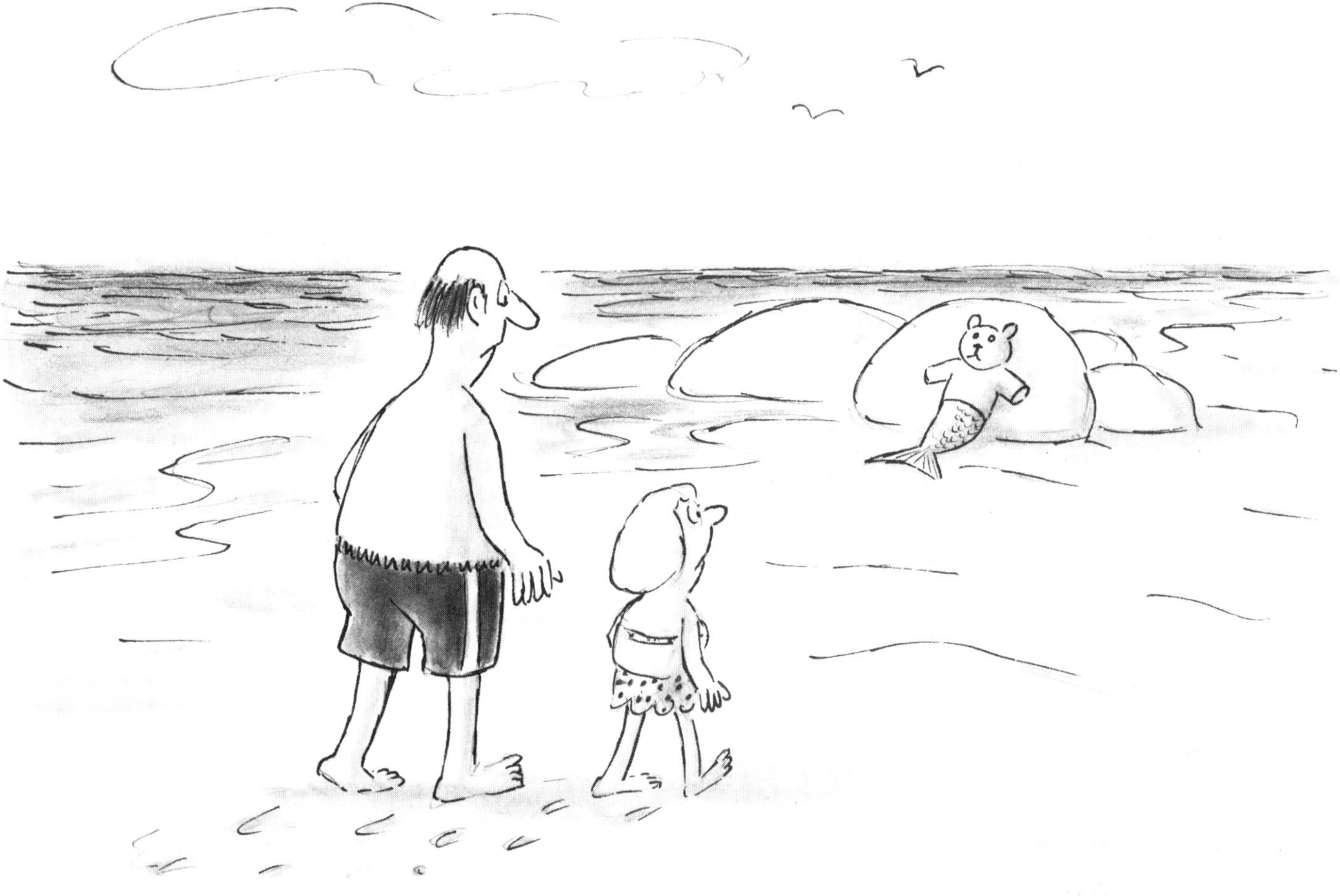

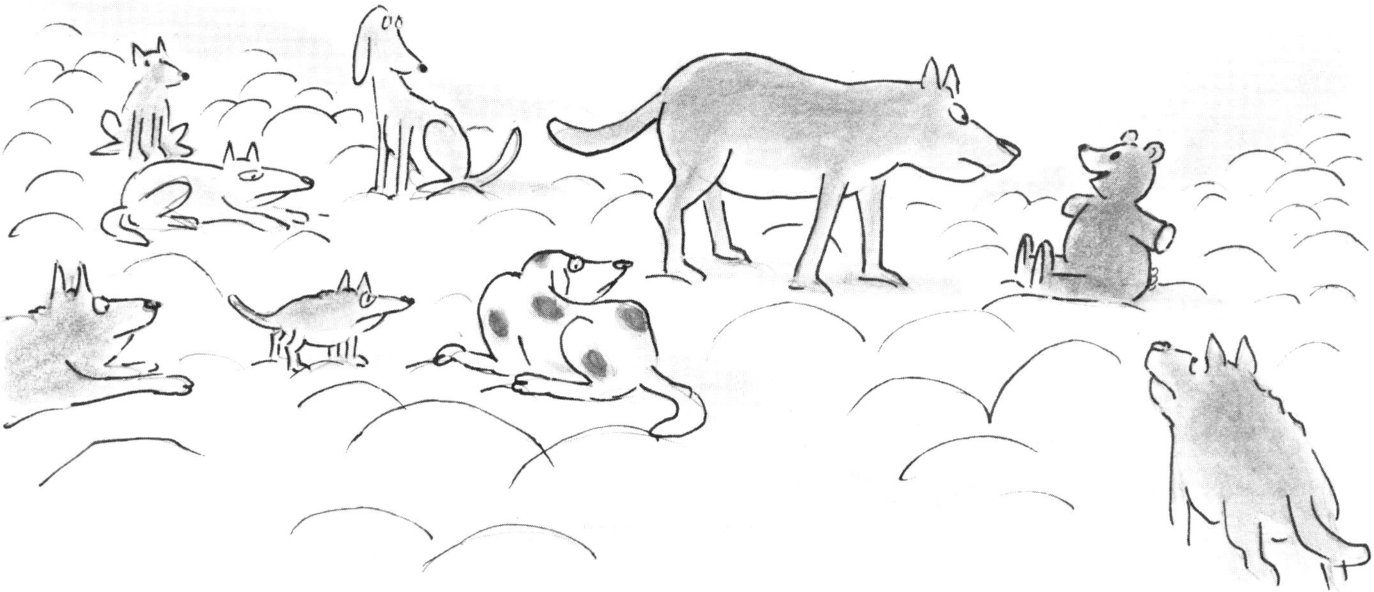

"Since there isn't a teddy bear Heaven, God made me an honorary doggie."

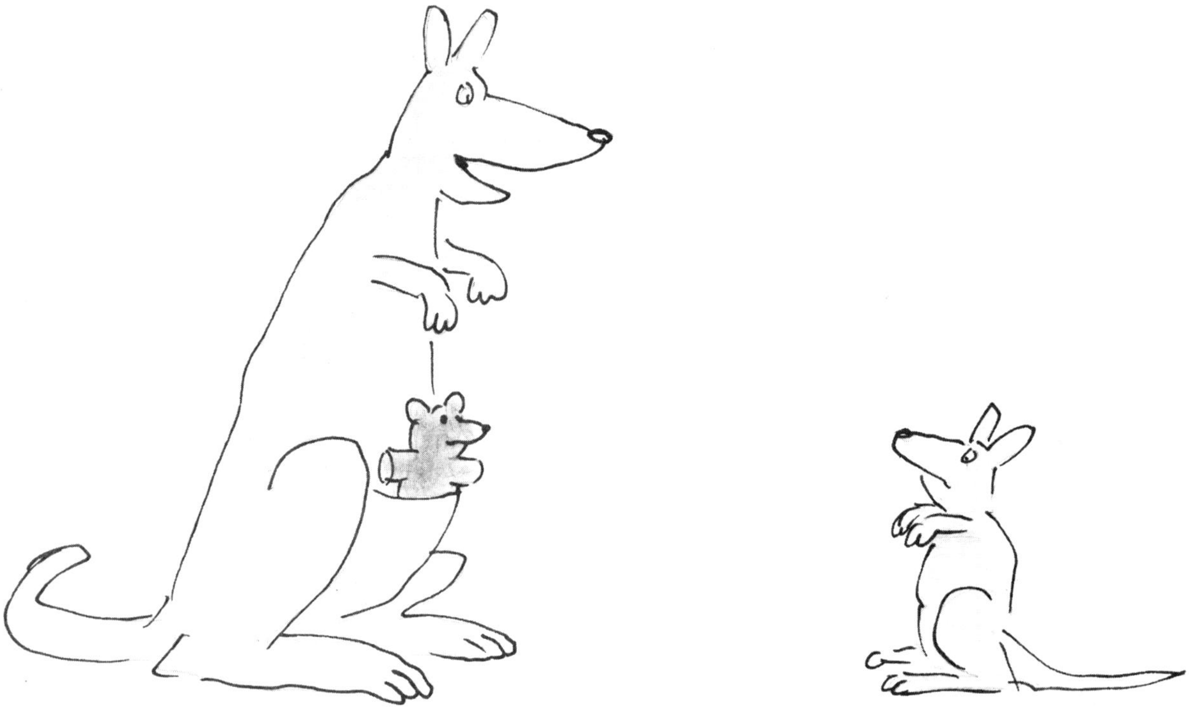

"I knew you'd be back when you realized you forgot 'Snookie.'"